THE TRACES

THE TRACES

AN ESSAY

Mairead Small Staid

DEEP
VELLUM
Dallas, Texas

A
STRANGE
OBJECT
Austin, Texas

DEEP VELLUM   STRANGE OBJECT

Published by
A Strange Object, an imprint of Deep Vellum
Deep Vellum is a 501c3 nonprofit literary arts organization founded in
2013 with the mission to bring the world into conversation through
literature.

This is a work of nonfiction, but memory is fallible and some names have
been changed.

Library of Congress Cataloging Number: 2022019611

ISBN 978-1-64605-200-4
ISBN 978-1-64605-201-1 (ebook)

Cover design by Kelly Winton

Interior design and layout by KGT

PRINTED IN THE UNITED STATES OF AMERICA

for my mother
for my father

No one, wise Kublai, knows better than you that the
city must never be confused with the words that describe it.
—Italo Calvino, *Invisible Cities*

CONTENTS

THE TRACES

CITIES & MEMORY

Y OU COULD SAY I missed a place. You could say I missed a time, or a place and time, or the person I was in that place and time—all of these sayings would be true. You could say I missed a particular season of a particular year when I lived in a city now thousands of miles away and many years ago. That distance widens by the hour, yet it amazes me that any time has passed at all. When I first learned to drive, I found it hard to keep my eyes on the road ahead instead of the rearview mirror—how entrancing it was, to see the past moving away from me at such speed. The sky and trees and buildings disappearing, and time made visible, physical, a set of measurements arrayed on the dashboard. Even now, I glance up—glance back—more often than I should, as if the road might turn to mist behind me if I don't keep an eye on it.

So I keep an eye on it.

In Italo Calvino's novel *Invisible Cities*, the explorer Marco Polo tells the emperor Kublai Khan about the many fantastical places he's seen: cities built of gemstones and illusions; cities sitting atop ladders and sunk into lakes; cities that disappear at sunset, remade each day. Through Polo's stories, Khan learns the customs and curiosities of the vast territories he has conquered; he learns the shapes of rivers and hills in the farthest reaches of his empire. In seeking to know them better, however, the emperor comes to understand the lands he claims to own as forever unknowable.

Polo begins his first report: "Leaving there and proceeding for three days toward the east, you reach Diomira." We are not told where *there* is. We don't know where we're coming from, nor what we've left behind, what we might see in our rearview mirror, could we glance at it. We begin in unknowing. Polo is less concerned with the past, whether of the city or the visitor to it, than with the interaction between the two at the moment of arrival. He speaks in the present tense.

One of the cities Polo has visited, however, is built by such backward-glancing, consisting solely "of relationships between the measurements of its space and the events of its past." But what does the traveler know of that past? The city "does not tell its past, but contains it like the lines of a hand." And the traveler takes that hand, shakes it in greeting, feeling the contours of the palm without knowing what they mean.

The city I visit is built of marble and limestone, water and air. Florence's past began under Roman rule, a military outpost of the sprawling empire. The city became a city-state, transforming time and time again under the sway of Romans, Ghibellines, Guelphs, the Medici, Savonarola, Machiavelli, the Medici again. In the midst of these shifting arbiters, the Renaissance rose and crested and fell away—though it lingers here, porous as yesterday. It lives on in the art and books, in the museums and classrooms, in the massive constructions of math and stone I pass by every day: the Duomo, San

Lorenzo, Santo Spirito. The Renaissance built the Florence found in my books and continues to build the city; it's the reason, after all, for my presence here—my footprints on the ghost of the Cassian Way, my own brief leavings.

I attend an American school on the southern side of Piazza Savonarola, the square named for a man who burned the books I love and was burned in turn. Inside, classrooms surround a green and flowering courtyard where I eat thin panini for lunch and drink espresso between classes, where I smoke cigarettes I've rolled myself, tobacco being cheaper by the bag and the satisfaction greater, I find, when inhaling something my own hands have made. Though I speak Italian with my host family, most of my classes are in English. I read Dante, Boccaccio, and Petrarch in translation, taught by a tall British woman who smokes copiously, leaning alone and elegant against the courtyard walls. My seminar on Leonardo da Vinci is led by a vigorous American expat, his face creased and tanned from decades spent under this country's sun.

I live a few blocks from school in an apartment with high ceilings and hardwood floors and my host parents: Mamma is a head shorter than I am, whip-thin, and skeptical; Babbo is tall, round-shouldered, and easily given over to laughter. It seems strange, at first, to call people who are not my parents *Mom* and *Dad*, even in another language, but I soon get used to it. I'm a child, after all, stumbling over simple words. I'm a child, being fed. Each morning, I wake to crisp biscuits and Nutella on the table, coffee and water ready to boil on the stove—all I need to do is turn the knob. Each night, I eat pasta and vegetables and meat dripping in sauces I can't name and will never taste again. Even as we eat lunch, my friend Annie and I have lengthy, long-ing conversations about what our host parents cooked the night before, what they might make next. We eat like crazy and are never sated. We swim through the days like catfish, taste buds covering our skin.

•

You can wonder about or if or whether, or you can simply wonder at. You can be full of wonder, the word turning from verb to noun, from action to state: a way of being. In Italy, I mostly do the latter. I stand before façades and frescoes with my chin uplifted, my notebook out. I write down facts and dates and anecdotes; I write down joy and want. I wonder at my own wonder. At my own happiness, which is near constant—I wonder at this constancy. (I do not wonder about, or if, or whether it will last.) I spend a single fall in Florence and will spend too many years to come attempting to reckon with those months. But what is there to reckon with? They happened; they—that is, the I who lived within them—happen no longer. This is how time works, a series of selves stitched together. *Oh my god*, I said to friends, upon returning, *it was the best time of my life*. I said this for a few months more, maybe a year, and then I stopped, though it hadn't grown less true.

In the bright light of early autumn, the Duomo gleams at the core of Florence, the massive cathedral larger by far than both the buildings clustered at its feet and the Apennines in the distance. To the south, the Arno catches the sun and tosses it skyward again. The river spindles through the city, splitting Palazzo Vecchio from Palazzo Pitti, the Uffizi from the Boboli Gardens, the marble *David* tucked away in the halls of l'Accademia from the bronze *David* pedestaled atop the hill of San Miniato, where he looks out over the Arno and the Apennines and the Duomo, etc. The city is as mirrored and lovely as one of Calvino's, and the great cathedral beats at its golden heart.

The Duomo took 140 years to build. The original blueprint called not only for the largest dome the world had ever seen, but for some as-yet-unknown method of support other than the flying buttresses of Northern Europe, deemed too ugly and Germanic for airy, glittering Florence. The Florentines wanted their cathedral to rise, light as wind, toward the heavens. They wanted their dome to *float*. "Even the original planners of the dome had been unable to advise how their project might be completed," writes Ross King in *Brunelleschi's Dome*. "They merely expressed a touching faith that at some point in the future, God might provide a solution, and architects with a more advanced knowledge would be found."

The best time of my life, I say, meaning *the happiest*. Almost three years earlier, I sat at a gleaming table on the bucolic campus of a boarding school, learning my first words of high-school Italian—*I have, I want, I need*—and felt my body shake from the force required to keep from crying. My first major episode of depression had arrived on schedule, just after my eighteenth birthday, and something in my body longed to get out, pressing against my skin with a deadening heat, sapping me of some strength I hadn't known I needed. I couldn't speak without choking up; it took tremendous effort to stand, to walk, to move from class to dining hall to dorm, where I couldn't talk easily with friends, couldn't laugh. *What's wrong?* my mother asked, when I called her sobbing, but nothing was. Nothing but a tightness in my throat and a numbness in my brain, a sense of awful exhaustion, of *wrongness*—all these nouns, with no verbs behind them. I left school to spend two weeks at home watching television and struggling to read even children's books.

Manic depression—which I have, in its mildest form—can be enticing, from the outside. The peaks and valleys of the disease lend themselves to metaphor: topographical, as in this sentence, but also seasonal, diurnal, thermal, weight-based. *My heart is heavy*, we say, *my heart is light*, as if gravity's effect were lessened when we stood on emotional heights, as it is on physical ones. From within, however, the metaphors grow futile. Depression reveals its dullness, less a deep cave or excavation than what it really is, in other contexts—a mere hollow in the ground—and the journey to its depths less a leaping plummet than a stumble.

But I didn't think this yet, in Italy. I was still enticed by those metaphors, even from within. I'd endured a third consecutive February wracked by depression, and summer too had been a struggle—listless, lonely—and now I was in Florence, in a golden fall, a where and a when that seemed inextricable, the beauty of the city and the beauty of the days braided together like water and rock. In my conflation of emotional states with physical ones, I began to associate the places I was depressed with depression itself, blaming a school or a city for my sickness. By this logic, happiness also became a place, a place I could visit, a place I wanted to live—and maybe that place was a city with a dome, with narrow, winding streets and sky-bright squares, a city just a train ride away from olive groves and sloping hills and a gleaming, unblemished sea. In Florence, I studied poems and paintings below oaken ceilings; I drank espresso in a sunlit courtyard. My heart was light, yes, and my mind felt keen and shining, a knife sharpened, after all the dull months, to a point. I found this feeling amid Florence's cobblestoned streets and marbled squares, and to those streets and squares I gave the credit. If I could only stay *here*, I thought, I could stay happy.

"But the special quality of this city for the man who arrives there on a September morning," Polo tells Khan of Diomira, our first destination, a shining metropolis of silver and crystal, "when the days are growing shorter and the multicolored lamps are lighted all at once at the doors of the food stalls and from a terrace a woman's voice cries ooh!, is that he feels envy toward those who now believe they have once lived an evening identical to this and who think they were happy, that time."

It's a hell of a sentence to parse. *Believe* and *think* imply a truth hidden behind false impressions; *now* and *this* and *that time* hint at a story beyond the page. This is the difficulty of beginning in unknowing—we continue in unknowing, at least for a little while. The original Italian is no less convoluted to this unskilled reader. Nearly a decade after learning to speak the language every day, to navigate train stations and post offices and friendship in this tongue, I can glean only the vaguest meaning from Calvino's sentences. In my broken-spined copy of *Le città invisibili*, an earlier self underlined in heavy pencil the words she didn't know—*lastricate, torre, accorciano*—the page studded with leaden evidence of all she meant to learn. She didn't, though—I don't know the meaning of these words. And I don't know nearly enough to untangle the knotted Italian grammar, the clauses within clauses that describe lovely Diomira.

Why does the man envy the others? Doesn't the sentence suggest that he's experiencing a true and present happiness, somehow more authentic (or so he feels) than that of those nameless others? Or is the traveler so jaded—he's seen the wonders of Diomira in other cities, Polo tells us—that no splendor can invoke happiness within him? I stare at the page for an hour and find no answers, just more questions. Why do the others only seem to recognize their happiness belatedly—*that time*? And why is the traveler skeptical of this recognition? I hear him scoffing in the line: *who* think *they were happy* . . . Why doubt that happiness? *D'esser stati quella volta felici,* concludes Polo's account of this first city, and the line, in Italian, lands on the very *felici* it would call into question. Why, above all, that question? What difference exists between thinking oneself happy and being so?

The prosciutto we should be piling into sandwiches is impossibly fine, as thin as silk or the flakes of paint missing from so many frescoes; our tongues grow clumsy under each piece. Annie and I eat our makeshift lunches outside Museo Nazionale di San Marco, a friary-turned-museum. Inside, the walls of each cell bear frescoes painted by Fra Angelico in the fifteenth century; each monk's room contains a masterpiece. I take a picture, not of Angelico's paintings but of a glassless window, looking south. The sky is white beyond the dim walls of the friary, and the Duomo rises into the frame, its dark dome stark against pale clouds. I've seen this improbable dome from a distance, walking the long street that leads from Piazza Savonarola to the city center; I've stood under it and wrenched my neck, staring; but this is a new angle, a surprise at the window. In Florence, the Duomo strikes me like the eyes of a painting, following its watcher everywhere she goes.

The more advanced architect, in whom the Duomo's original planners had placed their touching faith, was clockmaker and goldsmith Filippo Brunelleschi, who poured eighteen years and immeasurable invention into the structure I walk past each afternoon. The Duomo remains the largest brick-and-mortar dome in the world today. Seen across the rooftops of Florence, the cathedral is an adult thronged by children or a giant rising, head and shoulders above its human counterparts. It is closer kin to the mountains in the distance than to any of the manmade structures kneeling at its feet.

I'll learn, years later, that one isn't simply homesick for Florence. Instead, one suffers *la malattia del duomo*, the sickness of the cathedral, as if the Duomo towering over the city, almost twice the height of any other structure—builders even lowered streets around it to make the edifice appear more imposing to approaching visitors (like me, like you)—were the sole cause of this aching despondency, or the cure for it. As if all one missed were the building, as if the building were all one needed to be whole again and happy, and perhaps it is. No one calls it by its full name (il Cattedrale di Santa Maria del Fiore) but by its title, a duke ruling the rest of the city. For years, I'll assume *duomo* is simply a cognate, meaning *dome*, the building's uppermost and most striking feature standing in for the rest. A whole able to be represented, justly, in parts.

The Florence I describe in these pages is the Florence I saw as a visitor, as Calvino's traveler, and bears little or no resemblance to the Florence you would find should you travel there, nor the Florence inhabited by its residents, in which children grow up and the elderly die. My Florence held no death, no birth, none of the usual demarcations with which we attempt to rein in untamable time. Missives from the country I'd left behind hit like rain on a windowpane, unfelt and only partially seen, refracted by the glass of Italy. Everything there connected—the paintings, the writings, the mountains, the dome—and everything elsewhere served only to bolster the intricate web of thought forming in the poems I wrote, in the theories I had about art and beauty and travel and joy. My mind—have I said?—felt on fire.

We grow used to seeing ourselves in certain places, doing certain things, acting in a certain way. Our episodic memories accumulate, forming semantic ones: I did, I did, I did, therefore I am. We define ourselves by repetition, our persons—our personalities—formed like a portrait, brush stroke upon brush stroke slowly taking the shape of a cheek or a hand. We are creatures of habit, sure, and of habits, good and bad.

But the stories we like to tell are of exceptions.

You probably know this story: a twenty-six-year-old Michelangelo Buonarroti carved *David* from a single battered block of marble abandoned to the elements by an earlier sculptor, untouched except by sun and wind for thirty-five years. This rough, massive material was known to local artists as "the Giant," and Michelangelo (so the story goes) didn't carve the statue but *released* it, shearing away the surroundings of what was already there: the man had always stood, fully formed, within the stone. Michelangelo's contemporary, Giorgio Vasari, claimed that *David* so far surpassed all other statues, classical and new, that one needed to see nothing else to understand the sculptural achievements of the Renaissance.

Traditional iconography depicted David victorious, with Goliath's fallen head at his feet, but the young artist chose to excise Goliath entirely from the scene. Viewers can glimpse the giant only in their imaginations, a thing hulking at the end of David's long and steady leftward gaze. This particular David is pre-victory, pre-legend, a man staring down a monster thinking only, *How the hell?* And Michelangelo answers: his David is a giant too—*the Giant*—a Goliath of a man. He's not the boy of the Bible nor of earlier renderings: veins swell in his outsized hands and arms, muscles strain against their marble enclosure, and he stands almost seventeen feet tall. The top of my head doesn't reach even the plinth on which he lives.

The statue changes the story. Gazing up at *David* in the polished halls of l'Accademia, I think not *How the hell* but *How could he not?* Goliath didn't stand a chance. In 1991, however, a museumgoer tried to defeat the victorious David, removing a hammer hidden in his jacket and striking the statue, shattering the second toe of the left foot. Officials were able to collect the broken fragments and repair the foot, and I can't remember, now, if I noticed anything strange when I saw it seventeen years later. "A description of Zaira as it is today should contain all Zaira's past," Polo tells Khan, speaking of another city, and it's a worthwhile reminder, if an impossible task. For every visible seam of marble, another might lie hidden; for every statue mended, another might have shattered and been swept away.

•

What difference exists between thinking oneself happy and being so?
The question is part of a larger inquiry into the nature of happiness:
What *is* it? Is it something found or something made? Can happiness be measured, in degrees or length or weight, dense as marble
or airy as the underside of a dome? Can it be caught in words? Can it
be made to stay? Why does it attach itself to a place, a time, and not
let go? Why can't I let go in turn? And why is happiness suscepti-
ble to these claims of illusion, its veracity doubted? *Are you happy?*
we ask our friends, our lovers. *Are you really happy?* Calvino's traveler questions even the happiness of strangers, even the happiness
of moments long gone. Our memories of happiness grow dreamlike,
the silly, fickle, all-too-human gods of absent centuries, and in the
past, as in the present, we are unbelievers. We see the happy—others or ourselves—and we think, *Fools.* We bear them no allegiance.

In the shimmer of dusk giving way to darkness, Annie and I walk
with newfound friends down Via Capponi, past the tall apartments
and walled gardens. We pass through Piazza della Annunziata,
where a gravel-voiced man rasps in our direction—"Ragazzi!
Marijuana!"—and we laugh, sliding by, giddy *ragazzi*. The man
will be there every time we pass through the piazza after darkness; every time, he'll speak those words and nothing else. Though
I don't speak back, he becomes as essential to my Florence as the
David or the Duomo: another side of the city, a ballast, the shadowed corner of a painting that throws the rest into greater light. I
am not foolish enough, these months in Florence, to think myself
more than a tourist, but I am indeed foolish enough to think that
maybe, someday, I might be.

On Via dei Servi, we duck down a stairwell into a dark bar.
Our small group doubles the population of the place, a low-slung
room dotted with a dozen round tables, most of them empty, and a
small stage on which a man plays guitar and sings, in English, with

great feeling. The song is Prince's "Purple Rain," and the man is the bar's owner and booker and, two or three nights a week, performer. He's happy to meet us, he says, having finished his set and joined our table—he loves Americans, American music, everything. His English is far better than our Italian and always will be, but we try anyway, having a halting but effusive conversation in two languages. One of our friends is a musician, from New York—upstate, but he doesn't correct the Italian's thrilled assumption ("I *love* New York, what a city!")—and the singer speaks to him with the comfortable fervor of a fellow acolyte.

"This is what we try to do, yes?" he says, leaning over our wine glasses, eyes shining in the near-dark. "Make what we show on stage who we really are?"

In the hallway leading to the *David*, Michelangelo's *Captives* stand sentinel: originally commissioned for the tomb of Pope Julius II, they were never finished. Their arms reach out from blocks of marble, abdomens twisting against the stone, but feet and faces remain unhewn. Intended as symbols of the soul's imprisonment in the mortal body, the half-made statues—*who we really are*—serve the metaphor better than they ever could have completed.

Robert Coughlan, speaking of the more famous sculpture at the end of the hall, emphasizes the vast leap—generational, philosophical—that Michelangelo made in that single, massive, early work. "This David is not Hebraic but Greek," he writes in *The World of Michelangelo*, "not scriptural but Platonic." The young artist was a Neoplatonist, a believer in a high and perfect realm of which our own is merely a faint, flawed copy. His David is not the boy of the Bible's story—he isn't meant to be—but an Ideal man, perfected, some castoff remnant of that other world. "The human soul came from this Ideal realm and still has memories of it, however dim," says Coughlan, and *David* strikes me, standing in the golden light of l'Accademia, like such a memory: my mind suddenly widened, holding more than I'd known, and then the lingering, the reverie.

But perhaps the *Captives*, unfinished as they are, as we are, are the more apt rendering of human memory. Half-made by nature and half-hewn, their features blur and fade. A little is sharply drawn, but much is suggested. Leading up to the *David* like earlier drafts or primitive ancestors, they're marked most distinctly by what separates them from that finished and more perfect piece; their failures—of precision, definition, surety—are writ large. What we have forgotten is a far more vast territory than what we can recall. We couldn't traverse even a fraction of it, could we find again its hidden gates.

"Proust says memory is of two kinds," writes the poet Anne Carson in *Float*. "There is the daily struggle to recall / where we put our reading glasses // and there is a deeper gust of longing / that comes up from the bottom / of the heart // involuntarily."

You can imagine which kind interests me. But these facts and statues, these dates and domes—they're not mere decoration. "This city which cannot be expunged from the mind is like an armature," says Polo of the meticulously arranged metropolis of Zora, "a honeycomb in whose cells each of us can place the things he wants to remember."

In the strict organization of Zora, Calvino builds an altar to the mingling of episodic and semantic memory, a place—in the brain, in the world—where lived events are interlaced with knowledge. His construction is a chest with many drawers, a box partitioned into sections, or many boxes, hundreds, made of oak and gold and steel and words. Or a street, let's say—a street named Via dei Servi—that contains certain buildings: a bar, say, and the stoop of an apartment next to the bar where one might sit to smoke, and a café across from that stoop named Paolo e Francesca, after the lovers cursed for eternity in the second circle of Dante's hell. The names of those lovers, their affair and their eternal punishment, reside in the mind not in ink but in the large, illuminated script of a sign above a door, seen through the soft haze of smoke blown from a hand-rolled cigarette. "Zora's secret," Polo says, and *Florence's secret*, I think, "lies in the way your gaze runs over patterns following one another as in a musical score where not a note can be altered or displaced."

But I'm afraid, so afraid, that as I grow distant from the city, I might yet forget the song.

In Florentine folklore, depression is caused by winter's *tramontana*, the biting northern wind that comes in over the Apennines. I'm slated to leave Florence before winter hits in full, but the *tramontana* will find me elsewhere in February, as regulated as a bit of Brunelleschi's clockwork.

"Desires are already memories," Polo says of Isidora, a city built of spiral stairs and spiral shells, of telescopes and violins. The traveler arrives too late, however, to this exquisite city, and though he can glimpse its wonders, he can't experience them. He reminds me of Coughlan's Neoplatonist, who remembers, however dimly, the Ideal realm, "and hence is bound to be dissatisfied with earthly, imperfect existence."

Elsewhere, after Italy, I felt such dissatisfaction. (*You could say I missed a place.*) Calvino tosses off the clause—*This city which cannot be expunged from the mind*—yet the whole of his book (and mine) hinges within it. Expunged: to be forcefully forgotten, a means of sparing one's self some pain by foregoing some joy. Sometimes, all of time seems such a balancing act. We are each, yes, a series of selves stitched together—but the seams show, sometimes faintly, sometimes threatening to tear. We're always choosing or having chosen for us: what to expunge, what to clutch. Is it better to rip willingly than cling to the fading fabric? I don't know—I've never been able to tear myself away, attracted as I am to that *deeper gust of longing,* to the stories, the exceptions, I like to tell.

Once upon a time, I traveled across the ocean to live for a season in a city made of brick and mortar, wood and marble, cobblestone and river and light. No one, wise reader, knows better than you that the city must never be confused with the words that describe it, but I hope you'll indulge a little description nonetheless. I can't help it. If I could only stay here, I thought—every day, every minute—I could stay happy.

If I could only go back.

CITIES & DESIRE

Perhaps this matters, in considering my happiness: I'm in love. The kind that begins in an instant, quick as a wink—in this case, he actually winks. The kind that begins as a crush and continues: I'm crushed and crushed again. Such insistence has a thrill to it, a pleasure: I've always loved having my blood pressure taken, the tightening cuff. We won't sleep together in Italy, won't so much as kiss in three months rife with wine and cobbled streets and the sweet Mediterranean beyond, below, around. He has a girlfriend back home, and I am too fearful to test that limit—I would like to say *too good,* but no, it's fear—and these facts keep us circling like prizefighters, sizing up the damage we might do.

But isn't that the moment the crowd roars for, the moment each loves most of all? Before the match begins, when anything might happen? Forget what I said before: Who knows what won't occur? I write in the present tense.

•

Outside the Museo Leonardiano in Vinci towers a sculptural rendering of the Vitruvian man, the man—or men, two men, with arms and legs outstretched at different angles—pressed together like paper dolls and enclosed in the many ribs of a rotated circle. Our art history professor, a thin, brilliant man near seventy with a sky-wide American accent, summarizes Vitruvius's belief: the geometry of the human figure proved that man was the most beautiful being in creation.

"Vitruvius wasn't that intelligent," the professor drawls, and Annie laughs. Annie convinced me to beg my way into this seminar on Leonardo—I'm the only student in the class not studying art history back home. I don't know what *quattrocento posture* entails or who Giotto is. When the others select one of the famous paintings for their presentation topic, I take the allegories and the rough sketches for impossible flying machines. I'll come to love the artist's notebooks more than the *Mona Lisa*—but who wouldn't?

The flying machines are the focus of Leonardo's hometown museum—the paintings, too pricey for this village attraction, are at the Uffizi or the Louvre or the National Gallery in London. We gaze instead at massive wooden wings suspended over our heads, the sketches of a Renaissance genius given modern, if immobile, life. This is more than they ever got in Leonardo's time, the professor explains: manifold as the artist's interests were, paper was as far as most of his ideas went. With the weary affection accrued by a lifetime spent studying the man, the professor rolls his eyes at the wings and the accompanying sketches. "Very clever," he says. "And *very* impractical."

Leaving Vinci, we bus to a foundry in Pietrasanta, where limbs of bronze and plaster fill the buckets at our feet, awaiting bodies. A foundry worker peels back a mold to reveal the statue within, a woman made of dark bronze by the artist Maria Gamundi. Annie nudges me, nodding to the pinups cooing on the far wall. The workers plunge another mold into a massive tub of water, steam pouring into the air and reddening the faces behind their beards. I'm not sure which—the statue or the pinups, the uniform metal or the photographed flesh—is more perfected, more Ideal than real, though I can guess.

Then we travel up, up the coast and into the mountains, so we can shiver in the marble caves of Carrara, where Michelangelo's *David* came from, and his *Pietà*. We don hard hats and listen to a guide detail how arduous the work: to get at the stone within the stone, to transport so many tons of rock without damage. In the cavernous dark, the marble looks gray and seamed with dirt— who knew or trusted enough to haul such heavy blocks out of the mountain and into the dazzling light? Another touching faith was practiced in this flame-lit, freezing darkness, as breath plumed and vanished from the quarriers' mouths.

The morning's fog has lifted, and the mountainside blazes as we drive away, continuing northward: Annie has asked the professor to drop us at the train station in La Spezia before the rest of the seminar goes back to Florence. We're headed elsewhere.

Before and between Marco Polo's descriptions of the cities he has seen—cities of labyrinthine traps or shifting skylines, cities abandoned to the winds or filled with faces vaguely known, cities within cities within cities—Calvino offers his own descriptions, of the conversations between Polo and the emperor Kublai Khan. "Newly arrived," Calvino writes, "and totally ignorant of the Levantine languages, Marco Polo could express himself only with gestures, leaps, cries of wonder and of horror, animal barkings or hootings, or with objects he took from his knapsacks . . . the ingenious foreigner improvised pantomimes that the sovereign had to interpret." In the preceding chapters, then, and in the ones to come, are we reading Polo's account of each city or Khan's interpretation of each wordless pantomime? How many translations stand before us, of language and experience and gesture and gut?

In another novel by Calvino, *Cosmicomics*, a character describes a thing she has built as "an outside with an inside in it." Reading Leonardo's notebooks, I encounter: "A good painter has two chief objects to paint, man and the intention of his soul; the former is easy, the latter hard." Or, in other words: *This is what we try to do, yes? Make what we show on stage who we really are?* We bare our souls, or their intentions, or whatever it is we hope will be mistaken for our souls and their intentions—or we hide them entirely, because we are fearful or calculating or simply unable, unable to translate the roiling mess inside us into something another can understand.

The day was cloudy in Vinci and Pietrasanta, but Riomaggiore glitters in the sun. Beyond the railroad tracks, between the houses, the Tyrrhenian Sea lashes the rocky shore. Annie and I climb the town's stone-paved road to find the hostel office. The woman behind the desk is the first person we've met, after three weeks in the country, whose English is worse than our Italian, so we get to practice. We are ecstatic. She leads us out of the office and farther up the street, our legs straining against the precipitous angle. The town, as in a fairy tale, has been carved out of the cliff's side. Our room—and we don't see anyone else in the building, so it feels like our house, our home—is as high, we can't help feeling, as one can go. A balcony looks out over the cobbled street, the teetering buildings, and the crashing, happy ocean below.

Our friend Vignesh and his roommate are meeting us here. Annie and I go to school with Vig, back in the States, though none of us knew each other well there—here, we feel as close as family. Vig is good-natured, down to travel and ready with laughter, and accepts our constant, sisterly teasing with aplomb. We tease him about his bulky, pickpocket-thwarting money pouch; about how slowly he walks, a laidback Californian trailing two Northerners; about how a well-meaning study-abroad counselor told him—Vig is barely taller than Annie or I, and far gentler—that he'd have to protect us girls, in Italy. *Our protector!* is Annie's regular greeting for him, and his regular response: *Yes, yes, don't worry, I'm here.*

They arrive on the evening train from Florence; Vig tows a rolling suitcase for the weekend trip, which we tease him about. Annie and I have been in Riomaggiore for hours now, have eaten focaccia with fresh pesto and drunk a bottle of wine, so we show Vig and his roommate to the hostel with proprietary pride: here is our balcony, our cliffside, here is the shop where we buy focaccia and wine. There is our hostel owner, with whom we speak Italian. There is our rocky coast, our very own Tyrrhenian. We eat pizza by the side of the carless street and the evening light—it's mid-September— lingers longer than seems possible, given the restrictions of our planet and its atmosphere.

"The Greek word *eros* denotes 'want,' 'lack,' 'desire for that which is missing,'" writes Anne Carson in *Eros the Bittersweet.* "The lover wants what he does not have. It is by definition impossible for him to have what he wants if, as soon as it is had, it is no longer wanting." Our own language puts it as plainly, welding two meanings together to form the word: *want* spins like a pendant at the end of a chain, now a noun, now a verb. "This is more than wordplay," Carson insists. "There is a dilemma within eros."

In the early novels of ancient Greece, this dilemma underpins the narrative form: two lovers wish to wed or are wed and have been separated; something or some hundred things keep them from each other; in the final pages, after much struggle, they succeed at last in union or reunion. The author, Carson tells us, must

provide and vary—artfully or not—the many impediments necessary to sustain the story, frustrating the lovers' desires just long
enough to fill a book. Though it collapses, inevitably, in the final
pages, "a sustained experience of paradox" is what these tales
provide; Carson likens the lovers' journey to those imagined by
Zeno. Desiring to be together, destined to be together, they spend
most of the story apart. "It is the enterprise of eros to keep them
so," says Carson. "The unknown must remain unknown or the
novel ends."

The week before, back in Florence, we'd left the dark bar
charmed—by the singer, by the songs, by the pathos of the empty
tables and the pride we took in filling them—and walked back
up the street, through the piazza, past the gardens and museums,
unseen, unknown. The others split off, one after the next, turning
onto streets that led to their own temporary homes, until I walked
alone with our musician friend, Vig's roommate—let's call him Z.—
whose host family lived across the railroad tracks behind my own
apartment, so that for him to walk me home was not out of his way,
not really, maybe by a block or two, at most.

When we reached my apartment, we sat to smoke; he pulled a
pouch of tobacco and papers from his jacket pocket, and I retrieved
a carton from mine—he hadn't yet shown me how to roll my own.
We smoked, and talked, our knees jutting toward each other in the
limited space allowed by the building's stoop. Such small and common things, my knees, but I grew keenly aware of them, tucked
into their jeans; and of my hands, the welcome interlude of cigarette between their fingers; and of my eyes, counting as if by their
will and not my own the seconds spent meeting his, the seconds
spent looking away. Our conversation wound through the basic
facts of our lives back home until it arrived at the destination we'd
been aiming for since our introduction—his wink, my laugh—a
few days before. Did I have a boyfriend, he wanted to know, and I
said no. I'd wanted to live fully in this foreign place, I explained. I

didn't want a distant relationship dividing my attention, so I'd broken up with my boyfriend of six months shortly before coming to Italy.

"Yeah," he said, exhaling smoke slowly into the thickening air between us. "I probably should have done that."

We rise, Vig and Z. from bunk beds and Annie and I from the queen bed in the center of the room, our sleep guarded by Christ on the cross and an oil painting of the Virgin Mary. The perennially sauntering Vig puts on a T-shirt adorned with the Flash, making us howl. We sit on the balcony, *our* balcony, legs stretched out between the rails, and eat Nutella spread on crisp biscuits for breakfast. Terraced olive groves climb the hillside across from ours; below, the peach-colored roofs of town tumble toward the sea. The sea—it is a jeweled and hand-cut blue. At this great height, a line from Jack Gilbert's "Failing and Flying" keeps running through my mind: "Everyone forgets that Icarus also flew."

Down we go, down the steps of our hostel and down the steep street into town, where we stop to drink espresso in the sun. As the road lowers and levels out, we follow it right, winding away from the buildings and cafés and emerging with a view, again, of the sea. Cliffside paths connect the five villages that—along with the surrounding forest, mountains, and water—make up Cinque Terre National Park. Just a kilometer of coastline separates Manarola to the north from Riomaggiore, the southernmost town.

This first and shortest stretch is called the Via dell'Amore, and the coupled names of vacationing lovers have been penned on the handrail, painted on the cement, even carved into the huge leaves of plants lining the path: *ANDRE & VALERIA. NANDO & MARISA. GAIA TI AMO BY MIKELE.* We take pictures of the autographed flora; of each other, grinning into the sun; of Manarola coming into view, pink and green and yellow buildings rising from—or are they sinking into?—the rocks on which they're built. Each town is an improbable outpost, a Mediterranean mirage. Three years after our visit, the Via dell'Amore and much of the rest of Cinque Terre will be damaged by flash floods and mudslides caused by torrential downpours. Several people will be killed. The path will remain closed as I write, though travelers can use an inland route to walk between the villages.

"Eros is an issue of boundaries," Carson writes. "In the interval between reach and grasp, between glance and counterglance, between 'I love you' and 'I love you too,' the absent presence of desire comes alive . . . The experience of eros as lack alerts a person to the boundaries of himself, of other people, of things in general. It is the edge separating my tongue from the taste for which it longs that teaches me what an edge is."

That edge, that boundary, that betweenness, is not interstitial but essential, in Carson's formula. Eros, by definition, can exist only as long as it remains unfulfilled—a lack, a want—so that the edge separating lover from beloved doesn't threaten eros but sustains it. "Sappho perceives desire by identifying it as a three-part structure," says Carson, "lover, beloved, and that which comes between them. They are three points of transformation on a circuit of possible relationships, electrified by desire so that they touch not touching. Conjoined they are held apart."

In this "paradoxical role," both connective and divisive, eros excels. It shines, illuminating. "The difference between what is and what could be is visible," writes Carson. "The ideal is projected on a screen of the actual." (Hello again, Plato.) This is how Riomaggiore feels to me, even now, even after: the desire with which I traveled—carried everywhere like a second, weightless bag—made and makes that beautiful place more staggering. What could have been still shimmers like a promise in those waves.

•

The edge separating us shifts as we move: sometimes just a foot or two of air, sometimes a dozen. The expanse of floor between our hostel beds; walls and doors; restaurant tables, with their place settings and courses; the tiny cups of espresso we lift to our mouths; our cigarettes and their lingering smoke; the sidelong spaces of benches, stoops, and balconies; occasionally—leaning in for a picture or reaching a hand to catch the other's attention, to draw it in concert with our own—just a millimeter of cloth, just the impassable and breath-held edge of skin. It seems impossible that such a border—fragile as it is, feverishly as we lean against it—will not fall. The landscape is too lovely, the wine too bright; it's only a matter of the hours between now and evening—if not today, tomorrow. I exist in a state of constant readiness, *electrified by desire*. This isn't merely a metaphor: our bodies sweat imperceptibly in the grip of heightened emotion, exuding salt ions that increase the conductivity of our skin. The body grows electric.

Outside a tiny restaurant perched high on the hill between Manarola and Corniglia, the boundaries of eros appear as wooden slats in a picnic table: we sit across from each other to eat olives, bread, and cheese. A fine length of wire mesh runs along the dark cliff beside and above us, keeping it from crashing down. Branches stretch between the metal rings, and Z. reaches a hand above his head to unhinge a lemon from their leaves. He gives it to me with a flourish.

Only an Italian, wrote Johann Wolfgang von Goethe, could have created the hands of *The Last Supper:* "In [Leonardo's] nation, the whole body is animated, every member, every limb participates in any expression of feeling, of passion, and even of thought." This is true of my host parents, true of the Italian teachers at school and of the singer at the bar. And though his Italian blood is generations old and watered down, it is true of Z.—I've noticed this about him.

(I've noticed most things about him.) His fingers twist as he talks, as if molding delicate sculptures out of the air, as if the words he is searching for are small birds flying by and he must form intricate, invisible nets to catch them. He does; he snares them; he proffers them to me, hand extended like a golden platter.

And I take them, I give them—for such effort went into their capture!—great meaning.

Near the end of *Eros the Bittersweet*, Carson imagines a city where there is no desire: eating, drinking, and sex are mechanical chores. The inhabitants do not give each other gifts or tell each other stories. "They bury their dead and forget where," she writes, concluding: "A city without desire is, in sum, a city of no imagination."

A city made entirely of desire, on the other hand—Polo has visited such cities. In each, the dilemma within eros manifests in different ways: one city contains a thousand miniature, more perfect, and unattainable versions of itself; another fulfills every desire of youth but can only be reached in old age; the skyline of a third city shifts as the traveler approaches, so that the beauty he glimpsed from afar slips away with each step he takes. "Longing, we say," writes the poet Robert Hass, "because desire is full / of endless distances."

A kind of desire is mapped, too, in the very structure of *Invisible Cities*: though Polo soon learns Khan's language, able to deliver his reports in words instead of pantomimes, those early gestures haunt the relationship between emperor and messenger. In their limitations, in their very failure to be understood exactly, Polo's hands had spoken an essential fact. Words, after all, are just another set of gestures, whose meanings we think we have agreed upon. Distance is built into them. As Carson's lovers are connected and divided by eros, Polo and Khan meet and can never meet in the words they speak. *Conjoined they are held apart.*

"Back and forth across the edges [of language] moves a symbolic intercourse," writes Carson. "As the vowels and consonants of an alphabet interact symbolically to make a certain written word, so writer and reader bring together two halves of one meaning, so lover and beloved are matched together like two sides of one knucklebone. An intimate collusion occurs." The intimate collusion of Polo and Khan's conversation transforms over time: When the emperor misses the initial, gestural renditions of his empire, Polo forsakes language for his previous pantomimes. When those pantomimes grow opaque, Khan asks again for the reassurance of words. The emperor's desire shifts with what he's given, remaining forever out of reach; an edge is omnipresent, the third and dominant force in the conversation between these men. As their intimacy deepens, that boundary grows only more—or is it less?—solid and uncrossable:

> The Venetian knew that when Kublai became vexed with him, the emperor wanted to follow more clearly a private train of thought; so Marco's answers and objections took their place in a discourse already proceeding on its own, in the Great Khan's head. That is to say, between the two of them it did not matter whether questions and solutions were uttered aloud or whether each of the two went on pondering in silence . . .

> Kublai Khan interrupted him or imagined interrupting him, or Marco Polo imagined himself interrupted, with a question such as: "You advance always with your head turned back?" or "Is what you see always behind you?" or rather, "Does your journey take place only in the past?"

> All this so that Marco Polo could explain or imag-
> ine explaining or be imagined explaining or
> succeed finally in explaining to himself that what
> he sought was always something lying ahead . . .

Z. and I sprint the 368 steps that climb into Corniglia while Annie and Vig laugh from below, refusing to rush. We descend along the cliffs and into Vernazza, through Vernazza and down at last to the shore of the sea we've been following all along. The fifth and largest of the *cinque terre*, Monterosso al Mare sits more broadly than the rest, its main street parallel to the shore and horizontal. To walk on flat ground feels uncanny after a day of ups and downs, like stepping off a pitching boat onto a destined but not entirely welcome shore.

Here the ocean isn't backdrop but foregrounded: a beach runs the length of town, and we cross the strangeness of sand to swim in the last of the afternoon light. Tucked away at the center of a small gulf, the water of Monterosso is almost as calm as a lake or pond, far from the booming consummation of Riomaggiore's waves and rocks. Floating, I don't feel wearied by the day's hike but encased by it, as if my skin has absorbed the sun and sweat and kilometers like nutrients, and been strengthened by them. When Vig is stung, maybe, by a jellyfish—we examine the blush rising on his skin with the knowing air of doctors—we tease him for it, for his proclivity to mishap. We aren't worried. How could we be?

Dinner is pizza and wine on the patio of a gleaming restaurant, our swimsuits soaking through our clothes and onto the benches on which we sit. A string of baubled lights hangs above our heads, wrapped around rafters open to the sky, and the sea beyond grows gray, then black, then some other color entirely, as the sun sets beyond the next curve of the mountainous coast.

•

Eros is ever messing with time, heightening moments even as it has-
tens their conclusion, slowing and speeding our days at will. Eros
promises the eternal—*always*, we say, *forever*—but is infinite only
in its denials, its inherent and paradoxical dilemma. "No one in love
really believes love will end," Carson writes, and that *really* trips me
up, robbing me of any surety, any cynical confidence: How could
I possibly know what I believe, overcome as I am? In the ancient
poems Carson studies, eros is a destabilizing and violent force: an
enemy, wounding the lover's body, or a parasite, wriggling within
and taking control. As Sappho writes, in fragment 31: "cold sweat
holds me and shaking / grips me all, greener than grass / I am and
dead—or almost / I seem to me."

Despite this hostile takeover, we look *forward* to seeing the
beloved, to being in their presence. Our days become not happenstance but crafted: peaks and valleys, moments of encounter,
beginnings and middles and ends, which are only (in the course
of desire) another kind of beginning. Eros transforms the standard
progression of time into something more, something like a story. We
craft narratives around our beloveds, ourselves, and the meeting of
the two; the possibility of change—of plot—is constant. If nothing happens—no meeting, no kiss, no more—well, the story simply
continues. We'll wake to its delights another day.

In an essay, "You Need Not Doubt What I Say Because It Is
Not True," the writer Marilynne Robinson wonders if "depression may be the inability to sustain narrative." It's not merely the
angst, sorrow, and deep apathy of depression that dismantle me
each February, but the inevitable sensation—depression's ever-
present shadow—that this angst, sorrow, etc., will never end. That the
story will never alter, never surge, that there is, in fact, no story. In the
thick of it, depression is inescapable, no dark tunnel or deep water but
the whole of a small and ugly world, the only one you'll ever know.

"Do you think it's true that we'd never be unhappy if we never wanted anything?" one character asks another in Richard Linklater's *Before Sunset*. "I don't know," the other muses. "Not wanting anything—isn't that a symptom of depression?" She laughs, hollow and knowing: "It is!" These characters, I should say, want each other deeply, and have endured a separation to rival those of the ancient romances. Their conversation, like so many conversations, both prolongs their separation, making it a gradual matter—words first, bodies later—and relishes its imminent, inevitable end. "I feel human when I want something more than just basic survival needs," the woman says. "Wanting, whether it's intimacy with another person or a new pair of shoes, is kind of beautiful."

These lines rise to mind, as clear as—clearer than!—scenes from my own life, as unconsciously and as urgently connected. It's impossible to separate my time in Italy, or my memory of my time in Italy, from the idea I had and have of what my time in Italy was or is or should be. This idea is woven of many threads, and to cut even one would cause the whole thing to sag and gape. Prominent among those threads are the works of art I loved before I went, and still: Linklater's films of a couple speaking on European streets; Gilbert's poems set in Greece and France and Denmark, often about his former lover, Linda Gregg; and her poems about him. In these poems and movies, the act of embracing a foreign place is inextricable from another, bodily embrace, from falling in or out of love; every landscape is filtered through desire's lens.

Time wins out in the end, of course: eros dies, or its practitioners do. But who's to say, if this is yet the end? And now? Can the story still be happening, if it's being told? It's amazing, the way I feel *greener than grass* all these years later, a shiver in my body and a sense of excitement, of what might happen: though long separated from its source, the feeling is easily recalled—not merely remembered, but refelt, as if Sappho's shaking has been embedded in my bones.

•

The next day, we swim in the rocky surf of Riomaggiore and scrape our stomachs, hoisting ourselves back onto the slabs of marble that jut from town to sea, an unsculpted pier. Annie befriends an Italian swimming alone nearby, and we insist that we're going to leave her behind when we return to Florence: she must stay with this man, she must marry him, and then we can always have a home here to visit. I take a picture of Z. leaning back, bare-chested, against the rocks and the water beyond; another of him leaping, sky below his feet. He takes my camera to catch me playing on a marble outcrop, pretending to fall, and then approaching, the wind blowing my hair back and my sundress against my legs.

"For desire is like the secret of the suffering of a work of art, dispersed over the surface of the beloved's body, residing everywhere and nowhere at once," writes Carson in *Plainwater*. "I came on this trip to videotape desire—to obtain cheap, prompt, and correct facts about an object to which nothing in the world exactly corresponds."

One more pizza eaten on a roadside bench, one more bottle of wine, our hair damp from the swim. The weekend yawns and we have to go back to Florence, but it seems inconceivable that we won't return, and soon. *Dispersed over the surface of the beloved's body*—but it leaks here, my desire, adding droplets to the endless sea, shining in the air, coating the leaves of plants on which others have scrawled their want more plainly, without shame. I swim through it as thickly as the water.

Or perhaps—you've guessed this already—the osmosis works in reverse, the beauty of the place making him more beautiful, my longing to stay here, to stay *there*, grasping after any unknown and unknowable thing, any broad back and winking smile. Isn't that how the story goes? Doesn't the traveler find what she hadn't known she'd come looking for? Isn't that the reason for the book, the life—love in an unexpected place?

Some other book, perhaps.

"Desire is a moment with no way out," Carson says. The moment happened; the moment happens. "How can they say / the marriage failed?" Gilbert asks, indignant, amazed. They, whoever they are, have forgotten the way light can pour through another person, can ignite their presence, absence, presence again. A body can be heated and cooled as quickly as bronze, pulled from fire and plunged into ice. *To shiver*, as I did in the caves of Carrara, is the body's response to fear, to threat of exposure and threat of death, but also to anticipation, to excitement.

"Each one of us is but the *symbolon* of a human being," claims Aristophanes in Plato's *Symposium*; Carson explains that the word meant, in the ancient world, "one half of a knucklebone carried as a token of identity to someone who has the other half." In his famous dialogue, Aristophanes defines love as the result of a terrible severing: long ago, humans took a different form than the one we know. Our ancestors were rounded, he says, almost circular, with four arms and four legs and two faces, one on each side of the head—as if Vitruvius's rendering captured a single instant, and the man had another face, unseen but beloved, behind the page.

These ancient humans were strong and powerful enough to dare an attack on the gods themselves. Faced with this threat, Zeus devised a way to weaken his enemies: he sliced them in half, severing each human into two. (We have just two arms now, two legs, one face.) Now, Aristophanes explains, "each one longed for its own other half and threw their arms round each other, weaving themselves together, wanting to form a single living thing." The image has persisted, transformed in poems and songs, an undying definition of an indefinable emotion. "Most people find something disturbingly lucid and true in Aristophanes' image of lovers as people cut in half," says Carson. "All desire is for a part of oneself gone missing, or so it feels to the person in love."

But no: nothing is missing in Riomaggiore, in Florence. I am phenomenally whole—it's the wanting that makes me so.

"At the end of three days, moving southward, you come upon Anastasia," says Polo, describing a city of concentric canals, soaring kites, and glittering gemstones. "The city appears to you as a whole where no desire is lost and of which you are a part . . . You can do nothing but inhabit this desire and be content."

At the end of three days, moving southward, we disembark in Pisa to see the tower bending toward the ground. We eat—out of doors again, under another set of soft and pulsing lights—and the building flickers in the distance, looming over Annie's head like a movie set made real. On the train back to Florence, full and sleepy and unspeaking, I sit next to Z. as darkness comes and goes outside the windows. A few inches separate us, gulfs of air, at our nearest and shivering points. And as it did on the stoop of my apartment, on the hostel balcony, on the benches beside the sea, as it will on the steps of a dozen cathedrals, in the sweating air of a hundred bars, my heart performs its thundering two-step—*Touch me, touch me, touch me*. It's inconceivable that it won't always drum such a beat, that this song could ever be separated from the one that keeps me alive.

If this wasn't happiness, you understand, it was both close enough and better than.

CITIES & SIGNS

THE CITY IS REDUNDANT[;]" Marco Polo says, "it repeats itself so that something will stick in the mind." Later, he offers an alternative: "Memory is redundant: it repeats signs so that the city can begin to exist." Redundancy doesn't help my memory of Italy but hinders it: cities blend together. A piazza remains, iron tables and chairs on the cobblestones, oiled bread and wine on the table, and a low sun glowing through the trees that reach from the square's distant edge. A church remains, the bright white sandstone of the street outside, the marbled steps, and the sudden darkness within, slowly growing light.

I say these things: sandstone, marble. I have no idea. How does anyone know these things? How does one recount whole days, whole seasons or conversations? I can remember fifty words, perhaps, with certainty. Fifty words of the three months that thrum most insistently in my blood. How little must remain of the rest, the years in which I was, somehow, less present.

It might be in Lucca, that piazza, or Assisi, Siena, Ravenna, Fiesole. We took the train from Santa Maria Novella most Saturdays, gliding away from Florence and toward some other, even lovelier place for the afternoon. Each city, then, seemed indelible; now, I have to check the distances and directions of my memory against the maps. Descending into Italy via the internet, confronted again by those narrow streets, those beautiful buildings, I keep expecting to see myself, face blurred but something—height, hair, clothes— distinguishable on the screen. *You are here*, the maps say, the ones made for tourists who wouldn't otherwise know that simple fact. Now, moving only my fingers, traveling only through pixels: *you were there*. I'm not sure if the phrase is laced with reassurance or with spite.

We visit three churches in a day, a dozen in a week; we stand in more apses than I've seen in years. The incense scent of my Catholic childhood guts me each time: the ancient mosaics, yes, the exquisite frescoes, yes, but I close my eyes and I could be ten years old again, in a Massachusetts mill town—ten and restless and bored, trying very hard to focus my wandering brain on God, whoever He might be. I wanted, honestly, to be a spiritual child. I wanted to feel Him in the perfumed air around me, to hear the certainty of His voice. I wanted to be good, but more importantly: I wanted my life to be meaningful. I wanted to be filled to the brim with the kind of significance I thought only divinity could impart.

In this particular church, Ravenna's Basilica of San Vitale, Byzantine mosaics of saints and angels guard the triumphal arches. Each evangelist stands sentry in a corner, the man depicted alongside his traditional symbol: John's eagle, Matthew's angel, Luke's calf, Mark's lion. In classical mythology, lion cubs are born dead and rise to life after three days—you can see why the symbol appeals. But in fact, cubs are merely born with their eyes closed, which is not the same as being dead. It's not even the same as being blind.

The Old Testament is represented as well: Abraham, Isaac, Abel, and Cain are in attendance and have been since the basilica was built, a millennium and a half ago. Christianity was the latest import from the Middle East, our professor explains, and it intersected with the Roman ideal of beauty as a cultural ethos. Hence—the professor waves his hand around. Sure. Hence these massive churches, wallpapered in mosaics. Hence gold as far as the eye can see.

Representation was on the rise, too: more symbols, more mystery. The highest point of the presbytery bears not Christ's visage but his emblem, a lamb, encircled in flowers. Palms, fronds, books, and animals—to read the story of these walls requires a translator fluent in signs. If only Polo were here. "On the day when I know all the emblems," Khan asks the explorer laying trinkets at his feet, "shall I be able to possess my empire, at last?"

"Sire, do not believe it," Polo replies. "On that day you will be an emblem among emblems."

There's an idea—which is to say, I've found the following written in an old notebook, though I don't know its source—that the entire life of our world, the entire sum of our lives and those of everyone we've ever known, our pasts and our imponderable futures, our planet and the stars that blanket it, from inception to apocalypse and everything in between—that all of this takes place, as it were, on the eighth day of Creation.

There's a joke somewhere in there about Mondays.

Mathematicians and philosophers have considered the problem of the universe since ancient times, writes physicist Carlo Rovelli in *Reality Is Not What It Seems*. They always arrived, however, at "two absurd alternatives—the absurdity of infinite space, and the absurdity of a universe with a fixed border." It was Albert Einstein who, like a great writer, found the third possibility between two more obvious conclusions: like the surface of our planet, which is not infinite but neither is it bordered, "our universe can be finite but borderless."

Einstein proposes a kind of curving of three-dimensional space, known as a "3-sphere," as the shape of this universe: two spheres, meeting along every inch of their surfaces, both surrounding and surrounded by each other. (*An outside with an inside in it*, and another outside within that.) An astronaut who set off through the universe in one direction would eventually (if we ignore the hard fact of his mortality) return to the place from which he'd departed, just as an explorer who walks across Earth's surface (if we ignore oceans) will find herself back where she began. It's hard to picture—at times, I think I almost grasp it; at times, my mind founders and must begin again. But Einstein pictured such a universe, and so, Rovelli reminds us, did another genius in another century.

Dante Alighieri's *Paradiso* describes the poet's third and final journey, from the peak of Purgatory's mountain up through the sequential spheres of heaven, through the shining ranks of angels, archangels, principalities, powers and virtues, dominations and thrones, cherubim and seraphim alike. From heaven's uppermost sphere, Dante can see other souls, fellow travelers, ascending even farther: "My eyes followed their shapes up into space / and I kept watching them until the height / was too much for my eyes to penetrate." Dante himself is transported by the blazing gaze of his beloved Beatrice "into Heaven's swiftest sphere," where he observes: "The parts of this, the quickest, highest heaven / are all so equal that I cannot tell / where Beatrice chose for me to stay."

In this borderless, spherical space, Beatrice reassures the poet: "By circling light and love it is contained / as it contains the rest; and only He / Who bound them comprehends how they were bound." *It is contained as it contains the rest*—only He understood how at the time, perhaps, but Einstein would develop a hunch.

•

You will be an emblem among emblems. There's no sign of Khan in San Vitale, but another emperor rules the walls: Justinian I and the Empress Theodora are depicted on either side of the apse. Haloed and robed in Tyrian purple, the Byzantine leaders stand as tall as the angels and saints around them. They claimed the imperial prerogative, to be transformed from living, breathing beings into symbols—though what they're supposed to symbolize I can only guess.

Dante also transformed himself from human to icon in the course of writing *The Divine Comedy*. It is vital, says my professor of Italian literature, to separate Dante the Poet, writing the words, from Dante the Pilgrim, journeying to hell and heaven and back. Who is speaking at any given moment, she asks, the author or the character? A past or present self? It's a hell of a trick to play: Homer didn't pretend he'd fought outside the walls of Troy; Milton didn't make himself a spectator at the Fall. But Dante insists—within the pages of his work—that he's seen the icy lake at the world's heart where Satan lives. He has glimpsed God himself in the Empyrean realm. He has spoken to the dead, condemned and climbing and ascended. *The Divine Comedy* is autofiction, told in terza rima.

"How my weak words fall short of my conception," Dante writes, attempting to describe the sight of God, "which is itself so far from what I saw / that 'weak' is much too weak a word to use." The difference between Poet and Pilgrim is measured in the distance between conception and sight, between the word *weak* and the truer, deeper failings of the poet's language when confronted with something indescribable. (And isn't everything, in the end, indescribable? *No one, wise Kublai, knows better than you* . . .) After a hundred cantos and thousands of lines, after the torments of hell and the trudging of purgatory, faced at last with a glimpse of God Himself, Dante tells his readers, well, you'll just have to take his word for it—whoever *he* might be.

•

He's buried here, in Ravenna, in a sepulcher built for him beside the Basilica of San Francesco. Dante was exiled from Florence in 1302, charged with corruption and threatened with execution by the political foes who'd overtaken the city; Florence's city council wouldn't revoke the charges for more than seven centuries. (They do so, finally, three months before I arrive.) I find it hard—harder than with Leonardo or Michelangelo—to think of Dante as a once-present person, as a human who *lived and breathed*, as we say, as if the two could be tugged apart. Blame the book. Poet and Pilgrim blur through the misty distance of centuries, and he becomes more myth than man, mere vehicle. Hard to imagine him waking, dressing, walking the streets of a Florence he loved more ardently than I ever will. Hard to imagine him exiled to Ravenna, working for years on the *Comedy*, hard to imagine his hands, skin and nails, writing the words I read. Skin and nails are long gone now, but his bones lie behind the marble tomb I approach as if to genuflect, penitent.

Probably, I should say. His bones *probably* lie here. The location of Dante's bones is a subject more hotly contested than most. Repenting of its callous treatment of a now-famous son, the city of Florence demanded the return of Dante's remains after his death. Ravenna refused, and the poet's exile from his once-beloved hometown became permanent. To this day, a vacant tomb awaits him in the basilica of Santa Croce, inscribed with a line from the *Inferno*'s fourth canto: *Onorate l'altissimo poeta.* ("Honor the most exalted poet.") The following line—"His shade that left is now returned to us"—is conspicuously absent from the cenotaph.

In the seventeenth century, Florence's pursuit of Dante's remains grew so ardent that San Francesco's monks hid the bones in a monastery wall, where they would remain, hidden or lost, until 1865. "The head was moderately large," reports the *New York Times* account of this osteal discovery, "broad at the temples, while, the base of the skull bears token of an equally large development." (Phrenology, another obsession with outer signs and symbols, had its heyday in the nineteenth century.) Restored to a freshly built sepulcher in 1867, Dante would occupy yet another resting place in 1944, when the bombs of World War II threatened to shatter any structure in their sights. His bones were buried in the center of the church's courtyard until December of 1945, when they could be safely reinterred. A plaque and vine-laden mound commemorate the spot, twenty months of the poet's presence enough to consecrate the space. I take a picture of the vines, though they cover nothing now but dirt.

In Lucca, the next weekend, we rent bikes to ride the circumference of the old city wall, a broad ribbon of pavement circling the town. Annie doesn't know how to ride, so we teach her, taking it in turns to relinquish our own vehicles and guide her wobbling way along a stretch of the path. When she only narrowly avoids collision with a regiment of elderly women, Z. reclaims his bike, Annie on the handlebars, and we race away from the flurry of scowls in our wake. We speed along a straightaway, and the sun-warmed wind bridles against the finite, borderless surface of my skin: my face, my forearms, my hands releasing the bike, now, to rise into the air.

"Arriving at each new city," Polo tells (or imagines telling) Khan, "the traveler finds again a past of his that he did not know he had." Calvino continues in this vein: "Marco enters a city; he sees someone in a square living a life or an instant that could be his; he could now be in that man's place, if he had stopped in time, long ago." But there is no stopping in time; there's no stopping time. Time is not the wall around the city nor the basilica's dome, not circle or sphere or river or braid. Time is just another dimension, as Einstein knew, one in which we move—or rather, which moves us—only forward. "By now," Polo admits, "from that real or hypothetical past of his, he is excluded; he cannot stop; he must go on to another city, where another of his pasts awaits him."

In Assisi, we descend narrow stone steps to the crypt below the Chiesa di San Francesco, where St. Francis's bones are buried. Christ on the cross repeats endlessly in these churches, museums, and monasteries, drawn and painted and sculpted a thousand times and a thousand ways. In Assisi, the crucifixion scene is accompanied by letters: *IHS*, meaning *in hoc segno*. In this sign, rendered in the Latin I've long forgotten. In high school, I took classes in Latin more days than not, and though only a few years have passed since then, most of the language is gone along with them. I remember little of what I read then, myths and speeches and histories of the lands through which I travel now. Once, I'd read Virgil, Cicero, and Ovid—*I warn you, Icarus, fly a middle course*—but I'll have to reread Ovid in English a decade later; I'll have to learn again what I once knew. I'm always having to learn what I once knew.

Ancient pilgrims believed the air around a saint's bones to be curative, and pilgrimages to crypts like this one were not merely occasions for prayer: visitors came in search of health and blessing. Poor pilgrim that I am, am I after anything else? We leave Francis to his rest, ascending from the flicker of candles into sunlight, and climb a snaking path into the hills above the church. We claim the too-small swings of an empty playground, sending our bodies skyward, backward, skyward again.

In Siena, we buy bread and cheese and splurge on wine corked in the hills nearby. The surrounding towns bear names we know only from labels, and we pore over our maps, wondering if we might find a way out to the vineyards themselves, to the heart of Chianti. Carless, with limited hours, we can't. Our Italy is made of cities and the trains between them. The vineyards come to us instead, in long-stemmed glasses or sipped straight from the bottle.

We shed our jackets in the unseasonable heat and picnic on the sun-warmed brick of the Piazza del Campo, Siena's central square, where horses race the perimeter twice a year: dirt is shipped in to cover the brick, to permit a mad dash of dust and muscle planned for months, lasting for seconds. Z. leans back, jacket tucked under his head, and opens his eyes only to take the bottle I offer and lower it, carefully, to his mouth. I wonder, sun glinting in his beard and in the glimpses I catch of my own hair when it blows across my face, if there might not be a life somewhere in which every day is spent this way, wasted so exquisitely.

In her preface to *Eros the Bittersweet*, Anne Carson considers Franz Kafka's story, "The Top," about a philosopher who loves to catch children's spinning tops, mid-motion, as they play. "Beauty spins and the mind moves," Carson writes. "To catch beauty would be to understand how that impertinent stability in vertigo is possible. But no, delight need not reach so far. To be running breathlessly, but not yet arrived, is itself delightful, a suspended moment of living hope."

Desire doesn't hold a monopoly on this hope; the metaphor works literally, too. The delight of suspension can be found in physical travel: I ran breathlessly, in Italy, from city to city, from day to day; I didn't live in Florence long enough to catch that absent breath. I arrived every morning, every night; I was always arriving, was always not yet arrived. *What he sought*, Polo understands, *was always something lying ahead*. Perhaps this, then, was the source of my happiness: not the place itself, but the motion. Perhaps the best route to such happiness lies not in the backward glance of memory nor in desire, looking forward, but in this third possibility, this movement through space as well as time, this movement of the body as well as the mind. Beauty spinning, the cities shifting, and three months twirled like a top.

Back in Ravenna, another church. San Apollinare Nuovo was dedicated in 504 by Arian believers, a group distinguished from the dominant theology by their credence that Christ the Son is not consubstantial with God the Father. Instead, Christ was created (like us) at a point in time (like us), though that point in time was before the creation of the world. The Arian Christ is the first and most perfect of God's creations, through which all else emerges.

The debate is, at a certain level, a matter of linguistics. Arianism makes its claim based on conversations Jesus had with his disciples and on Bible passages that distinguish the "unbegotten" Father from the "only begotten" Son. In a letter, Arius wrote of Christ: "By his own will and counsel he has subsisted before time and before ages as perfect as God, only begotten and unchangeable, and that before he was begotten, or created, or purposed, or established, he was not."

The belief was and is heretical, contrary to the official doctrine determined by the Council of Nicaea in 325. (The Nicene Creed was one I memorized and recited as a child at church, and its lines come back without effort: *begotten, not made, one in being with the Father.*) In 561, San Apollinare Nuovo was reconsecrated to St. Martin, an opponent of Arianism. The story goes that Pope Gregory the Great ordered part of the church's famed mosaics, depicting the Arian king Theoderic and his court, to be destroyed. The human figures were blacked out, but their surroundings remain: tesserae form columns and arches on a wall above the actual, three-dimensional columns and arches of the room. Where Theoderic and his followers leaned against a column or extended an arm in front of it, those arms remain: they can't be covered up without disrupting the rest of the image. Disembodied fingers, hands, and wrists linger on the mosaicked columns, fragments made of fragments.

Our English *symbol* comes from Greek's *symbolon*—that lover's half-knucklebone made into metaphor by Aristophanes. A half that represents a missing whole, hands that hint at a body erased, a presence standing in for an absence—but don't they all? Take my own body, for example, twenty years old and standing in San Apollinare, but serving as evidence of another body, ten or eleven or twelve years younger, sitting in the pews of a childhood church. And another body, and another, infinitely divisible: they trail behind—and before—me like shadows, these other selves, until I myself, my self, am but an emblem among emblems. Like Khan, unbelonging in his own empire; like Polo, ever arriving and departing; like Dante in exile, I am always after something else, some elsewhere or when. My presence and my absence chase each other, a revolving door.

Twenty-three autumns earlier, Italo Calvino died at Siena's Santa Maria della Scala, just a few blocks west of where I'll sit on the Piazza del Campo, sipping wine. Then a hospital, the building is now (what else?) a museum. We won't visit it—paintings have been set aside for the afternoon, the sky too sharp to ignore. I won't yet know the location of Calvino's last breath, anyway. He was buried in the seaside town of Castiglione della Pascáia; Gore Vidal wrote about attending this burial for the *New York Review of Books*, about the winding drive from Rome to the village, about the whole country in mourning. Of Calvino's last novel, *Mr. Palomar*, Vidal writes:

> Are we a part of the universe? Or is the universe,
> simply, us thinking that there is such a thing?

Calvino often writes like the scientist that his
parents were. He observes, precisely, the minu-
tiae of nature: stars, waves, lizards, turtles, a
woman's breast exposed on the beach. In the process, he vacillates between macro and micro. The
whole and the part. Also, tricks of eye. The book
is written in the present tense, like a scientist
making reports on that ongoing experiment, the
examined life.

"The eye does not see things," says Polo, my favorite of Calvino's
observers and observations, "but images of things that mean other
things." He's right about the layers of meaning interposed: I glance
across the room at, say, an armchair, and what I see isn't the chair
itself but light sourced from the gray sky outside and the softer lamps
within, light reflecting off the wooden arms and upholstery, traveling
across the field of space and time between that chair and this other,
where I sit, through the cornea of my eye, through the pupil and the
lens, meeting the rods and cones of my retina, moving as electrical
signals through the optic nerve into my brain—seamlessly, it seems
to me, a thing both constant and instantaneous—where it is recognized and named, this object I've come to know as *chair*.

This applies to everything in sight: the lamps themselves, the
sky, my books, another person sitting across the room, a distance
that seems suddenly unfathomable. This problem—and I do think
of it as a problem, as something to be solved—grows dizzying.
"Talking this way," Robert Hass writes, "everything dissolves." I
feel this dissolution like anxiety, tightening in my body, these signs
upon signs like a million tesserae scattered on the floor. The mosaic
they're meant to form, the solution, is the work of more lifetimes
than I have at hand.

But I'm misusing Polo's phrase. The explorer refers only to part
of a lengthy journey: "Rarely does the eye light on a thing, and

then only when it has recognized that thing as the sign of another thing: a print in the sand indicates the tiger's passage." Arriving at last in the city of Tamara, the traveler reads the city as he did the land: "Your gaze scans the streets as if they were written pages: the city says everything you must think, makes you repeat her discourse, and while you believe you are visiting Tamara you are only recording the names with which she defines herself and all her parts." Is it strange to say I feel this way, not about Ravenna or Siena or Florence, but about the world? At times, this universe seems like a book whose words keep me from seeing its pages, its cover forever hidden from view. The longing this sensation prompts is kin to that felt for another, yes, for his hands and his words, but the ache is so much greater, for I don't know—*I can't begin to imagine*, we say, and for once this is true—what it would feel like to have it soothed, what it would feel like for this particular bodily want of knowledge to brim and fill. It's unquenchable, this desire: a perfect, everlasting lack.

"The lover's real desire," writes Carson, "is to elude the certainties of physics and float in the ambiguities of a space-time where absent is present and 'now' can include 'then' without ceasing to be 'now.'" But physics is less certain than we might think. Quantum mechanics has discovered that electrons manifest only when they interact with something else, colliding or conjoining. The silly habit of always having a fixed position is merely an endearing quality of more substantial bodies, like ours. Given this, given Heisenberg and Dirac, given black holes and quantum loops, we might more aptly sum up the laws governing our universe as the *uncertainties* of physics.

The lover's desire, then, might not be so impossible. As Rovelli explains, Einstein's theory of special relativity concludes that between the past and future of a particular event, there exists an "intermediate zone" or "extended present," the duration of which increases in proportion to the distance from that event. In the same room or even the same country, this intermediate zone is mere nanoseconds, but it lasts a few full seconds on the moon and fifteen minutes on Mars. "This means," Rovelli says, "we can say that on Mars there are events that in this precise moment have already happened, events that are yet to happen, but also a quarter-of-an-hour of events during which things occur that are neither in our past nor in our future." They are elsewhere—*elsewhen*, I want to say, but I'd better leave the physics to the physicists. "We had never before been aware of this 'elsewhere' because next to us this 'elsewhere' is too brief, we are not quick enough to notice it," Rovelli writes. "But it exists."

The term obsesses me: an *extended present*, deepest and most urgent of my desires. (*Longing, we say*—Hass again—as in, to make long; as in, to extend unending.) I wonder sometimes if beyond Einstein's genius and vision, beyond his influence and innovation, we laypeople know and love the man for this hint of possibility diffused throughout his theories or what trickles down of them to us: the concept that somewhere—some elsewhere—the present moment we would clutch forever, could we only find a handhold, still exists. It is not past; it is not gone. My god, what an idea.

Christ is backgrounded by gold tiles in San Apollinare Nuovo; gold fills the wall behind Justinian in San Vitale. In Byzantine mosaics, the use of gold was meant to indicate a thing eternal and omnipresent, a place beyond space, a time beyond time. (It's an expensive thing, eternity, reserved for emperors and gods, who can afford it.) But the theories of physicists make it plain: there's nothing that is not space nor time, nothing that isn't spacetime. Space isn't merely what we move through but what we *are*, a fabric woven from interacting quanta. Some of those quanta are us. Others form a chair, a lamp, some books, the sky—all made of the same uncut cloth. This cloth, this space, curves and turns under the weight of matter, shaping a tapestry more complicated than we yet can grasp. (Though we can, yes, *begin* to imagine it.)

Massive and stone-made as Ravenna's churches are, the buildings aspired toward a kind of dematerialization, the professor says, the same dematerialization Dante describes in the final pages of *Paradiso*. The intention of these spaces, their architecture and mosaics, was to inspire a sense of the infinite. "'Infinite,' ultimately, is the name that we give to what we do not yet know," writes Rovelli, sketching the long tradition of science as a series of mistakes made and corrected, made and corrected again. What we do not yet know is—oh, the temptation to say *infinite*—a tremendous amount. It's always been so. Isaac Newton, the finest mind of his era and a few others besides (as well as a committed Arianist), didn't know what to make of space—he called it "God's sensorium." *Sensorium*: the entirety of a sensory system, or the parts of the brain that interpret sensory input, or the results of that interpretation, or the totality of one's immediate environment in a given place, at a given time, if such things can be given. "No one has ever understood what Newton meant," Rovelli admits, "perhaps not even Newton himself."

Certainly, I'm not equipped to try. But I can't help seeing space—and time, its fourth dimension, its brute appendage, its complicating factor—in the mosaics before me, the millions of tesserae combining to make a greater whole. They collide and conjoin; they form a field through which charged objects interact. There are so many moving and unmoving parts. It grows hard to parse infinite in fact from infinite in practice: these thousands upon thousands of tiles, patiently set by someone's hands, are, technically, countable. But I can only begin to imagine doing so, and then my imagination fails. They aspired to the infinite, those hands, and I would let the word remain.

•

I know these discoveries and theorems, these systems and formulas, the work of minds far brighter than my own—they're wondrous enough without being twisted to fit these sentences. But such are my own uncertainties, such are the mechanics by which my mind operates, is stimulated and soothed. The wealth of evidence in this case—the case of my exceptional happiness—is overwhelming, so I sort it into piles; I sketch connections; I invent alphabets of signs by which my life might be translated. In the seams between tesserae, I see the field between particles, I see the space between our hands and mouths, his and mine—charged particles don't attract or repel each other directly, you know, but through that field. *They touch not touching.* In the depths and heights of Dante's circles, I find the giddy loops we made around Lucca, the horses' ringing stampede at Siena's heart, the steps of Assisi descended, ascended, and the pilgrims we became in the thick incense of that air. I struggle to separate the wonder of my mind's firing from the objects of that wonder, the wonders themselves—aren't they enough? Why this love of signs and symbols, this need to make things into metaphors and write those metaphors down? I worry that it might be vital to resist this impulse. To confront a thing and simply let it be, let it symbolize nothing but itself. Under all this mess of metaphor lies the real. Why continue to clutter it up?

"But then, little by little, the design became so important that it carried the entire book," Calvino said once, in an interview, of *Invisible Cities*. "It became the plot of a book that had no plot." In a 1984 lecture, William Gass pointed out the echoes of Dante's work in this design of Calvino's: the nine sections, the guided tour. Late in their conversation, Polo and Khan speak of "the inferno," though they have also, surely, spoken of paradise: the paradise of memory, the paradise of desire, the many paradises of science and language, of departure and arrival.

"And I who was approaching now the end / of all man's yearning," Dante writes, "strained with all the force / in me to raise my burning longing high." I don't know why—this clutter, this accumulation—but like one of the Duomo's early architects, I possess a touching faith: it might yet carry the weight I want it to, might yet become a plot. I take a picture of the sepulcher—the Poet's bones, I trust, below—and add it to the file. I raise my burning longing high enough to see.

THIN CITIES

Three hours on the train, a harrowingly brief cab ride through the pounding streets of Naples, an hour stagnating in the stale air of the ferry's cabins—the summery clothes we wear are no match for the wind on the deck—a funicular ascension from port to town, a cliffside bus ride, and we arrive in Anacapri with just enough time to drop our bags at the hostel and walk, electric with waiting, with chill, with a touch of hunger, to the rocky shores of the sea in the final minutes of the day's light. We dive from the island's western side, swimming out toward that fast-falling sun as if we might yet catch it.

We don't. The long shadows of cliffs appear on the water's surface, and the lights shining from the shore behind us gain in strength as the sun fades. In the water to my left, Z.'s head and arms grow dark, a shape less and less discernible. I can't glimpse my own limbs below the water, and though I know where they must be—my arching feet, my splayed and searching hands—my body too feels prone to dissolution. We swim until the heat of our exhilaration fades and clamber out, cold but lingering, dripping seawater onto the rocky shore until every miles-wide streak of pink has left the sky. *Capri*, we say to each other, making jokes—the pants, the salad—but also speaking the island's name with reverence, like a word we have just learned, or only just now learned the meaning of.

Happiness was serious business to the ancient philosophers who lived and looked out on this sea from another shore. My dictionary defines *eudaimonia* as "happiness or well-being" and *eudaimonics* as "the art or theory of happiness"—my chosen field of study. The word was not always so simply understood, however: the *Definitions*, a philosophical dictionary written in the third or fourth century B.C., defines eudaimonia as "the good composed of all goods; an ability which suffices for living well; perfection in respect of virtue; resources sufficient for a living creature." (The *Definitions* also defines humans as two-footed animals without wings.) This pluralistic explication takes its cue from Aristotle, who uses the word prominently throughout his writings.

In his introduction to the *Eudemian Ethics*, Aristotle quotes an earlier thinker's inscription on the temple of Leto: "Most noble is what is most just, but best is health, and pleasantest the getting what one longs for." (*The getting what one longs for!* Impossible thing.)

"Let us disagree with him," says Aristotle, "for happiness is at once the most noble and best of all things and also the pleasantest." Setting forth from this premise, the philosopher's goal is manifold: to define the word, to defend its primacy, and to ask, once defined and defended, how a happy life might be acquired. Is one happy by nature or is happiness learned and nurtured? Can we habituate ourselves to happiness through training, or does happiness strike like a bolt from the gods: a divine gift, sheer good fortune? Inherent in these inquiries lies another, the question "of what of all that is found in living is desirable, and what, if attained, would satisfy our appetite."

•

It is early October, still warm enough to swim indulgently, though the nights come on quick and cool. *Indian summer*, we'd call it in the States, the origins of the phrase unknown and likely better left that way. In the many languages of Europe, such a lingering summer is attributed to old women, to poor men, to wanderers. The weather is itinerant as we are, never meant to last.

Z. and Vig and our friend Mike and I walk back up the quiet streets of Anacapri to our hostel. (Annie is in Sicily this weekend, an optional trip organized by the school that, I think, I couldn't afford, unable to convince the financial aid office back home of its relevance to my coursework. Or perhaps I chose Capri, regardless.) Z. and I have claimed the narrow beds closest to the far wall, and he jokes that we could push them together easily—only a foot separates their edges. I roll my eyes. We take turns rinsing the sea from our skin in the tiny bathroom and dress for dinner back in Capri. We dine outside although it is, truly, too cool now for such a luxury, and my wet hair chills my shoulders. We order the island's limoncello and sip its brightness slowly, pretending the summer hasn't gone with the sun.

For Aristotle, happiness—eudaimonia—is a complex and compound thing, a noun that acts as adjective and verb. "We must regard happiness as the best of what are matters of human action," he says, and this distinction—*of human action*—highlights a great divide between the happiness of Aristotle and that of his predecessor, Plato. Human happiness, to Plato, was a lesser imitation of Happiness-with-a-capital-H, another Ideal good of his Ideal realm, perfect and unattainable. Aristotle makes happiness not only attainable but actionable, less a thing to have than a thing to *do*. He is concerned with practicality. He doesn't want merely to define

a happy life—though pages are filled with that line of inquiry—
but to explain how one might implement that definition, how such
a life might possibly be lived. "The task is better than the state,"
says Aristotle.

Yet happiness is also the end, the aim, the goal, and so can only
be achieved once the race is run. "One cannot be happy for just a
single day," Aristotle says. "That is why Solon's advice holds good,
never to call a man happy when living, but only when his life is
ended. For nothing incomplete is happy, not being whole." Here,
clearly, much is lost in the inexact translation of eudaimonia and in
my own unskilled reading. But I find this philosophy of happiness
appealing nonetheless: the word turns like a contranym, its meanings cleaving. Happiness is the endpoint *and* the race itself, the finished vessel and its firing. (I have arrived, am always arriving, have
always not yet arrived, and never will.) How fine, the line where
one becomes the other. How lovely, to let the edges meet and bleed.

One of my favorite cities is a "thin" city, in Calvino's categoriza-
tion. The city of Armilla "has no walls, no ceilings, no floors: it
has nothing that makes it seem a city, except the water pipes that
rise vertically where the houses should be and spread out horizon-
tally where the floors should be: a forest of pipes that end in taps,
showers, spouts, overflows." Whether the rest of Armilla was never
completed or was destroyed in some catastrophe that the pipes,
somehow, survived, Polo admits he does not know.

The answer is both, of course, in this book like a maze of mirrors: every city exists in every way—reflected, refracted. Armilla
is the city that gives me the greatest pleasure, walking through it
in my mind, a place where possibility stretches both forward and
backward in time. You might prefer Sophronia, where the circus is
permanent but the banks, schools, and factories pack up and move
on at season's end; or Isaura, built so precisely over a subterranean

lake that not an inch differentiates the borders of the two, the city and the source. "Consequently," Polo explains, "two forms of religion exist in Isaura." Some citizens believe their gods live in the water below, but others locate them in the pulleys and buckets and aqueducts that bring that water to the surface, in the very act of rising.

We hand the oarsman our tickets and step into a rowboat bound for a place so strange it might be included in Polo's reports. The *grotta azzurra* is accessible only by a small boat and only when the tide is low: the entrance sits at water's edge on a steep cliff, the opening just a few feet high, sometimes, and sometimes entirely beneath the waves. We lean back as the oarsman brings us close, looking up: blue sky, blue sky, blue sky, and then dark rock, and then another light entirely.

When the emperor Tiberius moved to Capri for the final years of his reluctant reign, this grotto was his personal swimming pool. Statues of Neptune and Triton once stood along the walls, and while some stone remains have been discovered by divers and recovered from the cave's bottom, others likely linger in the seabed below us, buried like sailors in a saltwater grave. Now, as then, the impossibly blue hue of the water exists due to an opening in the cliff wall below sea level, a gap far larger than the one through which we entered. A small amount of sunlight comes into the cave as we did, skimming over the waves, but more is diffused through the water beneath us, the light rising from below. The result is this underground sea, as bright as a sapphire.

The place is uncanny and pristine, possessed with a hallowed beauty, and I'm overcome by the pit-bottom feeling of stumbling into a church service I didn't know was happening and don't believe in, surrounded by a grace that grows cold around me. I long suddenly for the horizon, the rampaging shift and sparkle of the open sea preferable to this monotone jewel. Or perhaps I'm simply disappointed by the low ceiling of the cave above us and cold, not merely metaphorically, now that we're out of the sun. I grow inexplicably sad. I feel, not for the first time, like a tourist; for the first time, however, this seems like something I should be more deeply ashamed of. I wish we hadn't spent the money, though it wasn't much. "Want to swim?" Z. grins at me, ignoring the guide's glare, but no, I shake my head, barely able to laugh, no, to sink into this too-bright blue would not solve the problem of its perfection, nor make me happy. I trail my fingers in the water beside the boat, but I cannot touch it.

The surest routes to our mutual goal, says Aristotle, are virtue, wisdom, and pleasure, "three things directed to a happy employment of life." (I try to map my own routes—memory, desire, the spun top of travel—but find them leading in different directions, a dialectic I can't yet resolve.) *Pleasure* is a noun—and one we, in English, often conflate with happiness itself—but Aristotle resists the possibility of pleasure as an abstract concept. Pleasure doesn't exist independent of circumstance, he says, but is attached to the specific activity that produces it, that is *pleasurable*. Some pleasurable activities, certainly, "are perhaps base in the abstract," but some are not: the chief good, Aristotle claims, is pleasurable, even if not all pleasures are good.

Even in his day, the concepts were confused: "All men think that the happy life is pleasant and weave pleasure into happiness—and reasonably too." The confusion remains: my thesaurus suggests "pleasure" as a substitute for "happiness," though not the other way around. Happiness has fewer viable stand-ins, as it should—if not as loftily as eudaimonia, the word still resists definition. So we fall back on the ease of *pleasure*, and let the philosophy lie. My resistance to this conflation betrays a desire to deny that equivalency, to shame my thesaurus. Perhaps it's only a writer's impulse, to demand greater exactitude of the words I use when used by others, or perhaps it's a selfish wish. Immersed in my study of eudaimonics, obsessed with both the word and what it stands for, I can't allow the object of that obsession to be reduced to only pleasure—silly thing. *Wisdom*, Aristotle says, and *virtue*, and I cling to the thinning pages.

"You walk into the sunlight / to make yourself happy," writes Eleni Sikelianos in *Make Yourself Happy*. "This is the poem that will tell you / how to live." We walk—or are rowed, rather—back into the sunlight and to the shore, where we bid our guide goodbye and climb stairs cut into the rock face. We decide to forego the central beaches near the island's ports for the cliffs we found the night before, now intimately known.

In the full light of the afternoon, we're no longer alone at the rocky shore: Italian couples spread towels below their tan limbs, and families shout at each other in a language we can half—exactly half—understand. A group of little girls, each three or four years old, runs up and down the cliffs in their underwear, calling to each other at each fresh discovery: the chill of the water, the crevices in the stone. The sun's reflection in the Mediterranean is so bright, and so much closer than its cause, that I can't look directly at it, either. The water sparkles like snow or heaping treasure, a sea of diamonds instead of brine. I can stand its shimmering blue, can enter it.

We skirt the small cove and clamber up rocks across from the sunbathing families, where an outcropping juts from the cliffs, ten feet above the sea. Vig windmills his arms and legs, goofing; Z. backflips, heedless; I leap forward as far as I can, flung open all the way to my fingertips. The water's surface arrives like an exhalation, when I didn't know I'd been holding my breath. Vig and Mike have rented goggles and snorkels from a shop nearby, and we take turns submerging ourselves in the crystalline inlet, ducking under the soft waves to face the open sea, staring out and out and out to where it does not end.

The afternoon, too, seems endless. The couples have stopped talking and turned to sleep; the gang of little girls has disappeared around the rocks on another adventure. "When I came home," writes Sikelianos, "there were buds on the lemon trees and big light fisting through / the window—nothing / happier." I hoist myself out of the water and gather my towel, notebook, and cigarettes, taking them back to the outcropping to sit above the sea. Summer has come back with the sun, and I stretch my bare limbs under its light, feel my wet hair warming. I try (and fail) to ignore Z.'s gaze from across the water, try to remain within my body instead of without. I write down that trying, that failing, and smoke two slow cigarettes, drying my lips along with my limbs. I write: *I am made simply happy, the proximity of water and rock all I require.* "Some take to be parts of happiness what are its indispensable conditions," says Aristotle, though I don't know it yet. My trouble, I'll come to think, arises from the opposite impulse: I take to be indispensable conditions what are only parts. I circle and circle, but the whole eludes me. I glimpse just one city at a time.

The philosophers who came after Aristotle amended his definition of eudaimonia. For Epicurus, pleasure alone composed happiness, and other qualities—virtue, wisdom—were merely means to a pleasant end. For the Stoics who followed, virtue was the supreme quality and sole constituent of a happy life.

Aristotle, preemptively, is having none of these reductions. "Both the general run of people and the refined say that [the highest of all goods] is happiness," he says, but "the former think it is some clear and evident thing, like pleasure or riches or honor— some one thing and some another, and often the same man identifies it with different things (with health when he is ill, with riches when he is poor)." Hedonists and Stoics both, just the general run of people. Our refined Aristotle is after something else, something messier. My allegiance to him, however, isn't nearly so lofty. I'm wary of the hedonistic definition, reducing my precious happiness to cheap pleasure; I try to ignore the Stoics' dictum, which loads the word with a responsibility I don't want to bear. Pleasure, pain, longing, beauty, virtue—I'm twenty, and virtue is easily the least interesting of these.

Commotion on the other side of the cove. The Italian couples have roused from their rest, propping themselves on elbows or standing to peer into the glittering inlet. Families point and talk even more rapidly than usual, pulling their children from the water. I wave at Z., who stands at a little distance from the nearest family, following their pointing fingers with his eyes. "What is it?" I ask. He looks up, delighted. "Jellyfish," he says.

They are translucent as the glass he blows back home: small, clear bowls upended and pulsing in the sea. Jellyfish breathe by diffusion, their skin thin enough for oxygen to pass right through. The sunlight cutting through the water cuts through them just as easily, another exquisite refraction. Recipients and beneficiaries of the light, the jellyfish seem like its source: they glow like strung bulbs under the surface. They are too many to count.

A group of jellyfish is a bloom, a brood, a swarm, a smack. They begin their lives as planulae, small larvae which settle on surfaces—sea beds, floats, or boat hulls—and grow into polyps, their tentacles dangling upward instead of down. When ready—after a matter of years, sometimes—they detach from the ocean floor and rise, rotating, toward the surface. Though the largest variants swim in the open ocean of the Pacific, the Mediterranean is home to dozens of species, some harmless to humans, some not.

The jellyfish clustered in the cove are the size of my fist and colorless. If they have eyes—box jellyfish do, twenty-four of them—they aren't visible. The bloom hugs the cliffs fifteen feet from where I stand, now, rising to get a better look. *Nothing happier.* I fold my towel, tucking notebook and cigarettes beneath it, should a wind arise. My toes curl around the edge of the outcropping, and I don't leap, as before, but step gently, a single step out from the rocks and down, falling into the clear water that spans the space between us.

"If you choose to believe me, good." So Polo begins his account of Octavia, a city suspended over a mountainous crevasse like a spider's web. "[R]ope ladders, hammocks, [and] houses made like sacks" dangle below the precipitous walkways of the city, and below them, the clouds. "Suspended over the abyss, the life of Octavia's inhabitants is less uncertain than in other cities," Polo says. "They know the net will last only so long."

The "thin"-ness of these excerpts from Polo's travels is literal; the cities he visits are made of water pipes and pulleys, of stilts and spiders' webs. Stretched in various directions, they grow as fragile as malnourished bodies and, like those bodies, cannot be sustained. But Capri is thin to me in other ways. Capri is a city that's not a city, in anyone's imagination, but an island; it's a place taken since ancient times by the very rich for their very own, and I can't help coating it, as I do the rich, in a fine veneer of superficiality, of frivolity, of *pleasure*, in the word's worst sense, when I'm after something deeper, when I want a word by definition difficult to define.

And yet, I was abundantly happy there. But the distaste felt in the grotto (for myself, as well as my surroundings) hasn't left me; I can summon it as readily as the desire and wonder and delight. My happiness itself—gleaming and robust under that Italian sun, grown fat on food and art—was whittled thin in Capri, so thin I could look through it, translucent as the jellyfish. My happiness became brittle, as tenuously held as the city of Octavia. Or per-haps it had always been this way, and I'd simply been fooled again, mistaking a part for a whole, or a surface for what lay beyond it. Shouldn't I have known—so many Februarys already in my rear-view mirror—how fragile any happiness is? But happy as I was, I'd forgotten or ignored that knowledge, as if requisite to such happi-ness was the belief it wouldn't end.

"Is man naturally idle?" Aristotle asks. "Or as eye, hand, foot, and in general each of the parts evidently have a task, may one lay it down that man similarly has a task apart from all these? What then can this be?" By a process of elimination, Aristotle narrows the parameters of this task: it's not simply *to live*, for plants can do such a thing, nor is it to perceive the world through our senses—our sensorium—for animals can do that too. No, the quality unique to human beings is our reason, our intelligence, and our task is to make use of it. Happiness, Aristotle decides, is "activity of soul in accordance with reason."

Throughout Aristotle's consideration of eudaimonia, he uses sleep as a litmus test, an ultimate stand-in for inactivity, that bane of happiness. If the quality up for discussion is a state or posses-sion, and therefore can be had by our hero even while he sleeps, it's necessarily inferior to happiness, that superlative goal. Activity, whether of body or brain, is essential: the happy person circles, strives, pursues.

If we concede this point to the philosopher, no wonder depres-sion descends like a trap. Depression prevents doing; it's one of the disease's defining characteristics. When I'm depressed, even mundane tasks rise like walls. The idea of pursuing any loft-ier challenges, any *activities of the soul*—reading, writing, think-ing deeply—is unfathomable. This numbing certainty—not only that I can't read or write, think or do, but that I'll never again be able to—is one of the central tenets of depression. (I would call it a problem, but that implies it might be solved.)

So I like the joke embedded in the title of Sikelianos's collection: *Make Yourself Happy*, as if it were that simple. What a dream, that imperative. The poems within are full of wry suggestions, co-opting the easy, impossible injunctions of gurus or self-help guides: "To make yourself happy make / no error / ever // make no razor / mark let no / razor mark be made / upon you." The absurdity of the demand—*make no error ever*—highlights the absurdity of other, lesser instructions, the *chin ups* and the *snap yourself out of its*.

But Sikelianos is interested, as I am, in happiness disentangled from its opposite, happiness for its own sake. Let's set depression aside—there are more ways than the one to be not-happy, and they all pale next to the expansive blessing of happiness. Aristotle argues that happiness can be found in pursuit and achievement, and yet it's always seemed to me a more mysterious force, and one that comes on like the weather. I can go out into the downpour, can splash in puddles instead of skirting them, but I can't make it rain. "No one praises happiness as he does justice, but rather calls it blessed, as being something more divine and better," says Aristotle, and this falling back on divinity, unsatisfying as it might be, makes sense to me. Happiness is a fickle god all its own, and I've left so many offerings at its altar. "Happiness is among the things that are valuable and complete," Aristotle says, "an originating principle; for it is for the sake of this that we all do everything else."

Z. tosses me a pair of goggles from the shore. "Be careful," he says as I tug them on, treading water, and pull myself under the shining surface.

Eight months from now—on the other side of the ocean that fills this sea; on the other, rising side of a plummeting depression—I'll dive from a Cape Cod breakwater into a bloom of these creatures' cousins, there (as perhaps they are here) benign. I'll move my hands and feet more slowly than I thought possible, brushing their hundred bodies with a gentleness I've rarely felt, before or since. They will feel giving and resilient and somehow damp, somehow wetter than the water that surrounds me, as if visiting from some deeper sea. They will feel like grace. The moment will sear itself into my memory, an unforgettable—that is to say, unforgotten—joy.

In Capri, I keep my distance. "A space must be maintained or desire ends," says Anne Carson, and I don't shear a centimeter from the exquisite space between the bloom of jellyfish and me. (Eight months from now, I'll no longer be bothered with the maintenance—the exhilarating upkeep—of desire: I'll dive headlong into the bloom of jellyfish; I'll lift my lips to kiss the new man smiling down at me in the bar's dark. Of course, it's not that kiss-filled summer but this longing fall that occupies me still, not that time but this one that I can't stop wasting so many words on.)

In Capri, I don't need to touch the jellyfish to tremble. "To feel its current pass through her is what the lover wants," Carson says of eros, and what I feel, submerged in the Mediterranean, is akin to that electricity, its delight keeping me from the possibility of a more literal, less pleasurable jolt. I move as little as I can, only waving my hands as if to shoo the surface away. The noises above—the little girls are back, shouting at the sight of the jellyfish: *Medusa! Medusa!*—arrive as if from another world. I don't know how long I linger in this particular chamber of the sea, but the moment stretches, thin and lovely, in my memory: unforgettable, unforgotten. This suspension, this untouching, is an altogether different kind of joy.

"Happiness // is a form of it (*autopoiesis*)," writes Sikelianos, using a term coined by 1970s biologists to mean a system that produces and maintains itself, like a cell. "[I]s it recyclable?" she asks. "How many vowels do we need to mean it? What is the waste at the end of use?" Here is the end of this writing, if not all writing: to recycle my life, my happiness, to minimize its waste, to conserve its vowels. If we scavenge through philosophy and science, taking their words for our own purposes, aren't the laws of conservation terrifically happy ones? They speak of transformation without death, change without loss: less static energy simply means more kinetic; less energy, more mass. Nothing's ever truly gone. If my happiness produces and maintains itself, it hasn't disappeared, no, it must be merely hiding somewhere, hibernating, preparing to propagate again. This *autopoiesis*, this self-making—what else is autobiography? In the course of editing (less mass, more energy), we find a truer imperative, the serious matter behind the joking mask: the task is not *make yourself happy* but *make yourself.* Make your self.

It's a fine, self-serving tradition in which I take part. "That which is appropriate to each thing is by nature best and most pleasant for each thing," says Aristotle, "and so for man the life of the intelligence is best and pleasantest, since intelligence more than anything else is the man. This life therefore is also the happiest." How convenient, at the end of all his reasoning, that Aristotle finds the occupation of a philosopher most suited to the pursuit of happiness. And how wonderfully fortuitous, that this writer can conclude the same about writing.

Still, Aristotle keeps tripping me up: his obsessively rendered and repeated definitions, which seem, somehow, less certain every time he states them. His abstract concepts, deployed as if they were minor details. The contradiction at the heart of his eudaimonics, the lovely and unsolvable problems of time and death. After every concluding statement on the topic of happiness, he jots a postscript: "But we must add 'in a complete life.' For one swallow does not make a summer, nor does one day."

What difference exists between thinking oneself happy and being so? Aristotle's need for completeness provides an answer to this question, the one I find posed by the first of Calvino's cities. How can I be happy when I've not yet crossed the finish line? Silly me, that afternoon in Capri—sun in my damp hair, on my bare limbs, sea sparkling and my mind along with it, my breath going in and out like the tide and my body composing, composing—silly me, to think myself happy. To make myself happy. To write that happiness down.

TRADING CITIES

K UBLAI KHAN HAS GROWN distracted in the course of Polo's
reports. "Khan had noticed that Marco Polo's cities resembled
one another," Calvino writes, "as if the passage from one to another
involved not a journey but a change of elements. Now, from each
city Marco described to him, the Great Khan's mind set out on its
own . . ." Cities begin to build in Khan's imagination, spiraling and
plunging: minarets, alleyways, rivers, and docks; the calls of birds
and children; the scent of metal. Marco continues to describe the
cities he's seen, but Khan isn't listening.

"From now on," the emperor interrupts, "I shall describe the
cities and you will tell me if they exist."

I don't set foot in Turin, industrial center of Italy's jagged northern edge, but see it through the eyes of the book I carry through
a dozen other cities. Even now, train tickets sprout between its
pages: *da Firenze a Lucca, de Paris à Chartres*. I'd bought the
poems and novels of Cesare Pavese in preparation for traveling to

Italy but it's his diaries, collected in *This Business of Living*, that hum in my mind, that I quote aloud to Z., that I take for my own. I find the book in the bin of a used bookstore, broken-spined and yellowed along its edges, yellowed even—once opened—along its margins, each page a picture framed with wear and the warp of yesterday's sun.

Pavese was born in 1908 in Santo Stefano Belbo, a small village in Cuneo, the province bordered to the west by France and to the south by Liguria, where the Cinque Terre are hammered by the sea. To the north lies Turin, Italy's first capital, where Pavese attended school and university. "The place where you are really yourself is that avenue in Turin," he writes in the diaries, "noble yet unpretentious, broad, calm and serene, where it is always spring or summer and where your poetry was made." I read this sentence, and its companions, and experience the sensation of finding something so deeply felt—not needed, not even wanted, but a thing that encroaches on the margins of my life, leaving indelible notes—that the impetus is to insist that it found me, chance too meager a reason for such communion. We're always doing this, we humans: imposing meaning on coincidence, finding divinity in the vagaries of luck. Call it a narrative impulse, a psychological need.

This need exerts its influence on the past as well as the chancy present. Memories flutter and rise—a rainy night in Florence, splashing through the puddles that spread between the cobblestones, hair plastered to my cheeks and my sweater soaked, glancing back as I duck into some warm, dim bar to meet Z.'s smile—and even now, I smile back. But these details lack context, a scene without a plot. Where were we, and why, and what did we say? So little is left—these disconnected fragments like diary entries, and whole pages ripped away. ("Memory is an ugly thing," says Pavese, but its opposite can be just as gruesome.) What remains grows weighed and bowed, staggering under the burden of a meaning it was never meant to hold. It was just an ordinary, happy night, and if it survives in ways so many others haven't, it does so without divinity or intention.

In the centuries since Aristotle, eudaimonics has wandered from the realm of philosophy and been adopted by psychiatrists. Eudaimonia appears in modern study as *eudaimonic* or *psychological well-being*—as distinct from the lesser *hedonic well-being*, pleasure once again relegated to a second-class status. Psychological well-being was conceptualized in a 1989 paper as a six-part structure: autonomy, personal growth, self-acceptance, purpose in life, environmental mastery, and positive relations with others.

With apologies, these phrases arouse in me an unwavering desire to smash my head against the nearest wall. My precious eudaimonia, reduced to a to-do list. Discussions and definitions of happiness flourish in the sopping borderlands between psychology and self-help, and in neither platitudes nor academic prose do I find anything resembling those moments when the scrim separating me from the sky or the sea or this lamp-lit, book-filled room is lifted and the world gleams even when I close my eyes.

It occurs to me only now that my interest in psychology—I've always thought myself interested in psychology: buying books, reading papers—might be an interest in the object of its study, and not the study itself. An interest in happiness or insanity does not necessitate—and perhaps precludes?—a vested interest in the manufacture of that happiness or in curing that insanity. Perhaps I'm rooting for psychology to fail. In his cultural history of mental illness, *Madness in Civilization,* Andrew Scull writes, "Unreason continues to haunt the imagination and to surface in powerful and unpredictable ways. All attempts to corral and contain it, to reduce it to some single essence seem doomed to disappoint."

•

In Khan's declaration, another possible answer arises to the question posed by each page of *Invisible Cities*: Are we reading Khan's imaginings, now, instead of Polo's reports—or Khan's interpretations of Polo's reports, that is, or Polo's unspoken responses to Khan's interpretations of Polo's reports? The possibilities branch and splinter. Khan dreams of a city and Polo admonishes him—that is the city he was just describing. Khan dreams of a city and Polo out-dreams him, insisting that he has not seen Khan's city, he will never see Khan's city, the city does not, cannot possibly, exist. Khan dreams of a city set on a harbor, where passengers make their farewells in silence before boarding a tar-smeared ship, and he commands Polo to set off at once, to find this city, to bring news of Khan's vision back.

"There is no doubt that sooner or later I shall set sail from that dock," Polo says, "but I shall not come back to tell you about it. The city exists and it has a simple secret: it knows only departures, not returns."

One of the cities Polo does tell Khan about (or Khan imagines, or Polo intuits, or etc.) is Euphemia, where merchants meet on each solstice and equinox. By day, the merchants trade goods—fruits and nuts, fabrics and trinkets—but they also gather by fires at night and trade stories. "At each word that one man says," Calvino writes, "such as 'wolf,' 'sister,' 'hidden treasure,' 'battle,' 'scabies,' 'lovers'—the others tell, each one, his tale of wolves, sisters, treasures, scabies, lovers, battles." And when the merchants leave Euphemia, it's those tales, not their own, that they take with them, the memory of some other man's wolf or lover rising in their minds as they ride away.

In our own Euphemia, which varies from day to night and week to weekend—Riomaggiore, Ravenna, Lucca, Capri, the dappled benches of the school's courtyard, the bass-driven dark of the bar—I give Z. the words of Dante, of Pavese, of Jack Gilbert and Linda Gregg. I quote Federico García Lorca on *duende* and Walter Pater on Botticelli. In exchange, he teaches me to throw darts in the neon gleam of yet another bar, his hand arranging mine around the metal. He shows me how to roll cigarettes from the small bags of tobacco we buy on each Florentine street corner, both the regular method and the dollar trick, which makes the tiny cigarettes denser and smoother, less likely to wrinkle along the thinning lines where our tongues have licked them shut. He offers the basics of glassblowing, the landscapes of vineyards, Jim Morrison and the 27 Club. "Don't join the club," he'll whisper, months later, autumn giving way to winter and his breath warm against my ear, and the simple premise stuns me: that I might matter more than whatever I might make.

"Some may contend that the more a work tends toward the multiplication of possibilities, the further it drifts from that *unicum* that is the writer's self," writes Calvino in *Six Memos for the Next Millennium*, a collection of lectures and his final, posthumously published work. "On the contrary, for who are we, who is each of us, if not a combinatorics of experiences, of information, of things we have read and imagined?"

We can't meet each other in the ways we might prefer, Z. and I, so we fall back on the combinatorics that make us up, these things we have read and imagined. But no, *fall back* implies a demotion, when the heady barter of these months is no less weighty than any consummated romance. It might be more so: unable to put our mouths to better use, we have to talk. Unable to let our hands rest too long on each other, we have to point elsewhere, to scavenge the crashing ships of our lives for other things to offer. We have to gesture—in Italian, the word *gesti* means deeds or events as well as gestures. There's nothing empty about them.

•

"How happy she was," writes Pavese in the novel *Among Women Only*. "It seemed a miracle." How sad, I thought, reading these words, to think happiness so rare as to be miraculous, though I knew it could be true. But I think now that Pavese (or the character to whom he gives voice) doesn't mean that the presence of happiness is miraculous, but the degree. *How* happy she was. We don't ask this of others, nonrhetorically—*how happy are you?*—though I think perhaps we should.

In 1935, Pavese was arrested for his association with anti-Fascist circles and spent a few months in prison, then a year in internal exile in southern Italy. When permitted to return to Turin, he began working as an editor and translator for the publisher Einaudi. (It was in this role, a decade later, that he'd meet a brilliant twenty-four-year-old named Italo Calvino.) Pavese avoided enlistment in Mussolini's army due to his asthma and lived for a time in the Piedmontese hills while German troops occupied his beloved Turin. After the war, he worked for the newspaper of the Italian Communist Party (alongside the younger Calvino) and published poetry, fiction, and philosophical dialogues. "Above all," Calvino writes of his friend's novels, "they are works of an extraordinary depth where one never stops finding new levels, new meanings."

I keep finding new levels and meanings in Pavese's diaries, too; I find a man grappling with his own forming and unforming ideas. "Never doing as the serpent does," one early entry says, "never shedding one's skin: For what really belongs to a man, in life, except what he has lived? But keeping a balanced view, because what has a man to live for, except what he is not yet living?" Life hinges like a book, and Pavese often seems, in the diaries, unable to decide which way to read. He knows he should look forward—"The only joy in the world," he writes, "is to begin"—but the past obsesses him:

"I mourn for my past unhappiness."

"The richness of life lies in memories we have forgotten."

"We realize things are happening when they have already happened. You know now how full your life was in '45–'46. Then, you lived it."

I don't know if I buy it. I carried a notebook everywhere in Italy; aren't the hundreds of sun-stained pages in my hands evidence of a similar impulse in Pavese? We travel, talk, eat, drink, read, laugh, and think, and then—in the same instant, often—we write that thinking down. That traveling, that laughing. Such writing is an act of math, in my mind, adding another dimension to the figure formed by the scene: think of a line fragment hidden behind a point, a cube rising from a sketched square. This geometry functions as archeology, preserving not only the added dimension but the others, not only what is written but what inspired it—preserving the moment experienced both within and without as if in a safe, its code clearly written but decipherable only by its author.

But the memory, accessed via a scribbled note or not, is not clearer than or superior to the moment itself: Why else would we go to such lengths to make the moment stay, in any form? The moment is the masterpiece, the *David*, and memory is just the keychain imitation. Memory, in this case at least, holds no greater revelation: I knew—I think I knew—the import of each week in Florence even as I lived it. (Was this knowledge central to my happiness—a happiness rooted not in blissful ignorance but requiring and expanded by a constant, hyperconscious awareness of itself? Did thinking myself happy make me so?) Maybe Pavese would disagree. But it seems so clear to me, so horribly clear, that these memories, few and lacking as they are, cannot be the end, the pinnacle. To be awash in them, even bodily—I return Z.'s remembered smile; I close my eyes against the sun of Capri—pales next to the tidal pull of the real thing.

Of course, that pull itself is just a memory, and perhaps I cannot trust it. Perhaps what I've long thought were the many dimensions of an elaborate figure are merely trompe l'oeil. I have to admit the possibility that my memory, limited in so many ways, might have gotten it wrong in this one, too: maybe I wasn't *that* happy. Maybe such happiness, both intensive and sustained, isn't possible—is just another imagined city, never to be found.

I offer the story of Magdalene and *noli me tangere*, the starvation and the glut; Z. loans me the copy of *Girl with the Curious Hair* that he's brought with him to Italy. I go to college where David Foster Wallace teaches, back in the States, and Z. finds it unforgivable that I haven't yet read his work, let alone taken a class with him. ("I will," I assure him. "I will! I've been saving it for next year.") Z. loves Wallace, his fingers going wild as he tries to explain why. I take the proffered book.

"If you want, your whole life in the adult world can be like this country," says the narrator of "Westward the Course of Empire Takes Its Way." "In the center. Flat as nothing. One big sweep. So you can see right to the edge of where everything curves. So everything's right in front of your nose." I read this and think *yes*, in spite of Tuscany's hills. *Everything's right in front of your nose*. There it is: a description almost scientific, I think, in its precision, reduced like an equation—a description, a definition, of my happiness.

But the man who wrote those words wasn't happy, in the end. A few weeks after we arrive in Florence, a few days after Z. hands me a much-loved book, Wallace hangs himself in his garage in the college town I've so happily left behind.

"No one ever lacks a good reason for suicide," writes Pavese, in the diaries, but we're more likely to blame unreason for the act. Every variety of insanity—depression to schizophrenia, the lurid to the mundane—might cause a corpse. A suicide is the ultimate failing of psychiatry, the patient transformed from defendant to evidence, and yet psychiatrists persist: they might yet find a cure. In the meantime, suicide acts as a brutal metamorphosis, coloring the life that came before. In ancient traditions, according to Kay Redfield Jamison's *Night Falls Fast*, such metamorphosis occasionally was— or was believed to be—literal, altering the body after death. In Finnish folklore, the bodies of suicides were thought to be unnaturally heavy; in some Greek city-states, as postmortem punishment, "the hand that had been used for the act was severed from the arm."

In Dante's *Inferno*, suicides are the only residents of hell denied the use of their human forms. They appear to the Pilgrim as a forest of dark trees: "No green leaves, but rather black in color, / no smooth branches, but twisted and entangled, / no fruit, but thorns of poison bloomed instead." When Virgil, urged by Dante, asks one of these souls if there's any hope of regaining his body, the soul replies: "We shall return to claim our bodies, / but never again to wear them—wrong it is for a man to have again what he once cast off. // We shall drag them here and, all along the mournful / forest, our bodies shall hang forever more, / each one on a thorn of its own alien shade."

Dante's sympathy, aroused throughout the *Inferno*, surges here: he can't even speak to the souls in the trees, so moved is he. Pavese is less pitying, blunter and plain. "Here's the difficulty about suicide," he writes. "It is an act of ambition that can be committed only when one has passed beyond ambition." In my own notebook, I write just a single, fractured line on the topic: *DFW occupational hazard*. A childish thought, a clumsy and false thought, but I'm thinking of the graffitied plants along Via dell'Amore, their urgency, whimsy, and charm doomed to drop and rot. And yet the lovers' initials wouldn't be so striking, inscribed on a surface less inclined to dissolution. A week after Wallace's death, we visit the Gori collection of site-specific sculpture outside Pistoia, where an artist has uprooted stones usually embedded beneath Chianti's soil. Exposed to the air, the guide says, they'll erode rapidly: impermanence is built into the sculptures made from such material. Beauty and ruin (I think—childish, clumsy) intertwine.

I've since read most of Wallace's books, Z.'s tale of treasure or battle taken for my own. On my shelves sits a book he once owned: Wallace's copy of J. D. Salinger's *Nine Stories* was among those left in his office and bequeathed to my college's library after his death. It was given to me by a friend, an ex-boyfriend, who worked in the library, a man—though he seemed a boy to me then, as I was a girl—who'd once held me in the dark of his tiny dorm room and told me of his own suicide attempts. He was the first man I'd slept with, and I thought sex would always occasion such intimacy, like a password spoken by our bodies, opening doors within the other.

The paperback's spine is cracked like tree bark, a tear threatens to separate the back cover, and *DAVID WALLACE* is written in faint green ink atop the first page. The same green ink underlines words and sentences in "The Laughing Man," with minimal marginalia. No other story is annotated, not "Uncle Wiggily in Connecticut" or "For Esmé—with Love and Squalor" or "A Perfect Day for Bananafish," the collection's opening tale of travel and sunshine and suicide.

How happy she was. It seemed a miracle. I take the words for my own, copying them from Pavese's novel to my notebook, and their meaning slants with my handwriting. But in *Among Women Only*, this miraculous happiness is felt by a character only in the moment right before she loses consciousness, having overdosed. She is revived—her suicide attempt a failure—and survives to recount this happiness, if not to relive it. (*The city knows only departures, not returns.*) The novel ends with a second overdose of barbiturates in a rented room, another—more successful—attempt.

"For all men," writes Pavese, "the question of whether suffering is useful or useless must be determined in relation to their whole existence." We don't make such demands of happiness. Joy and delight, even simple pleasure—they are finished works, not the tools that build them. Teleology is inherent to Aristotle's understanding of eudaimonia, an end in itself.

But the longer I live immersed in this study, this hunt, the more I find myself questioning happiness: What use is it? What use *was* it? Perhaps a distinction lies in this issue of tense: in the midst of my happiness, it seems sufficient, more than sufficient—how could it not? Any deficiency would rend the fabric of the thing, unease creeping unforgivably between me and the sky that I swear, if I wanted to, I could reach out and touch.

Afterward, however, removed from my happiness and returned to my everyday moods (or worse), that absence emerges and persists like a blurring at the corner of my eye. I can't look at it directly; I can't shake the way it dims the world. Shouldn't such happiness as I have had leave more than mere residue, filmy and thinning? Shouldn't its effects be more lasting? The emphasis shifts once more: how happy she *was*, and is no longer. How happy, she is sure, she will never be again.

It's only in rereading Pavese's diaries that I realize my self-imposed course in happiness might have originated in these pages. The author, too, was obsessed with the emotion. "While we are in pain," he writes, in 1938, "we believe that outside our circle of suffering happiness exists. When we are not suffering, we know that there is no such thing as happiness, so we feel even sadder at having no pain to endure." Of course, he later counters his own argument. "Are you happy?" he asks himself. "Yes, you are happy. You have power, you have genius, you have something to do."

We know that there is no such thing as happiness. And Calvino, remember: *D'esser stati quella volta felici.* We don't question sorrow, anger, or envy in this way; we don't doubt the very existence of these emotions just because they've left us. Are they so much more indelible, more memorable, more fully felt? I don't think so; I think the opposite might be true. Why, then, is happiness so hard to believe in? Why is happiness so hard: to articulate, to create and recreate, to make linger and last?

"I should be perfectly happy if it were not for the fleeting pain of trying to probe the secret of that happiness, so as to be able to find it again tomorrow and always," writes Pavese. "But perhaps I am confused and my happiness lies in that pain. Once more I find myself hoping that, tomorrow, the memory will suffice."

The memory doesn't suffice. I'll spend the winter after Italy, the first few months of that fresh year, in another country far from mine, another city with gleaming streets and towering churches and a river coursing at its heart, a city soaked in myth and literature, a place where I could be—should be—happy, again and still. I'm not. The *tramontana* finds me within weeks and doesn't leave. I stop going to classes; I stop going out with friends to the city's twinkling bars. I do not want—anything, anyone—and whenever I try to convince myself otherwise, to habituate myself, as Aristotle might advise—*The task is better than the state*—back into the realm of the well and the wanting, when I let a handsome friend-of-a-friend follow me up the narrow stairs of my apartment, hoping I might find my happier self on the other side of desire, I discover just another colorless shade of my unease. It came on like a sickness, this itching in my throat and eyes, and stayed; I feel unhinged from my own distant skin. *I'm not myself*, I want to tell him. I want to plead my case before some unearthly jury, want this sentence, which seems endless, to be lifted—*This isn't me, the real me*—though what evidence do I have of that? Each passing day, eyewitness, says it is.

I'll leave that city two months earlier than intended, going home again: a surrender. Here's one reason why happiness might be harder to believe in, to remember or recall, than its many brutal opposites: it can leave little trace. My depression, on the other hand, is easy to corroborate: stilting emails to school administrators, the purchase of a plane ticket. Even the absences caused by depression are substantive, gaping holes: whole weeks missing between notebook entries, a dearth of photos in the middle of a well-documented year, and the empty spaces on my transcripts where the classes I can't bring myself to go to are declared, light with euphemism, *incomplete*.

Another kind of lack, that.

Once, before leaving, I run out of groceries—no host parents here—and spend a day and a half swallowing nothing but water and the bitter taste of cigarettes smoked by my cracked-open window, the cold blowing in. I've hand-rolled them, but this is a matter of frugality, now, not of pleasure. When I force myself out of the room, into my coat, trudging down the block to the corner store for bread and cheese and back again, I lie down on the stiff bed still in my coat and shoes. I don't rise for hours. The uneven white of the wall beside me begins to dim in the sunset of that short day, and continues: off-white, light gray, dark gray, darker. The light switch seems a mile from me. My limbs feel drained, of blood or muscle or some other anatomical necessity, and cannot lift. My mind would curse its own vacant shape—how empty, how ugly, this stupid mind in which I used to take delight—could it only find the words. It can't; I can't. I've left or lost them somewhere, far away.

The study of psychiatry is much older, as old as insanity itself, but the word only emerged in Germany in the nineteenth century. "It was fiercely rejected by the French (who preferred their own term *aliénisme*)," writes Andrew Scull, "and by the English-speaking world, which began . . . by calling medical men who specialized in the management of the mad 'mad-doctors.'" Mad-doctors since

Hippocrates have sought specific, bodily causes for depression and other mental illnesses: in Hippocrates's time, and for many centuries after, depression was thought to be caused by an excess of black bile, one of four humors believed to govern the body. Such an excess was also thought to cause or be caused by a heightened intellect, and this association of intelligence with madness persisted long after the humoral theory was laid to rest. "Scholar's melancholy" was a ready diagnosis of the Renaissance. During the Enlightenment, the image of the happy savage was contrasted with the woeful, knowledgeable, civilized man. And in an 1845 report, the State Lunatic Hospital in Worcester, Massachusetts, noted that "among the ignorant and uncultivated, the mental faculties lie dormant, and hence are less liable to derangement."

At the heart of these horribly flawed hypotheses beats a persistent idea: that mental illness conveys a certain character, that melancholy increases with IQ, that madness is not without its perks. Strip away the classist and racist underpinnings, and a wistful hope remains: it can't be all bad, insanity. Plenty fits under the umbrella of this wish: that suffering might be not merely useful, as Pavese surmised, but *necessary*, that pain might be not merely inevitable but, in a certain cast of light, desired—*an occupational hazard*, and a welcome one. In February of 1936, in the thick of what seems (from the pages of his diaries) like depression, Pavese writes, "I must learn to take this futile collapse, this wearisome uselessness, as a blessed gift—such as only poets can receive—like a curtain before the play begins again. A period of self-questioning."

Like an explorer on a drift expedition, I've let the current of my moods take me, rudder up, so that I might know and map their patterns. But that's not the only nor the foremost reason for my resistance (a common one) to medicating my depression. No, the hope remains: something might be gained from these months of misery, something that can't be found by any other means. In "The Artist as Exemplary Sufferer," an essay about Pavese, Susan Sontag writes: "As a man, he suffers; as a writer, he transforms his suffering into art. The writer is the man who discovers the use of suffering in the economy of art—as the saints discovered the utility and necessity of suffering in the economy of salvation." How fiercely this economy acts on would-be writers, this one included; how strong the lure of such transformation.

And I've succumbed, too, to the banal, embarrassing, and ancient belief that there's something *interesting* about madness and its attendant suffering, something far more fascinating—to art, to psychology—than health or happiness, dull old happiness, the province of pastel self-help books and treacly idioms.

Consider this writing the confession of a convert, and an attempt to make amends.

In another essay, "Camus' *Notebooks*," Sontag aligns the diaries of Pavese and Albert Camus, flattering neither: "They do not have the white-hot intellectual brilliance of Kafka's *Diaries*. They lack the cultural sophistication, the artistic diligence, the human density of Gide's *Journals*." I bristle, defensive. I first read Camus as a teenager, and it might have been his work, still fiercely loved, that prompted my self-education in eudaimonics.

"One must imagine Sisyphus happy," Camus writes in "The Myth of Sisyphus," his essay on the "one truly serious philosophical problem" of suicide. His conclusion rests on the small, almost silly feeling that obsesses me, that can't possibly bear the weight I want it to, so slender does it seem. And yet, Camus persists. "One does not discover the absurd without being tempted to write a manual of happiness," he claims. "Happiness and the absurd are two sons of the same earth." It's omnipresent in the essay, this absurdity, this happiness. "This word is not too much," he says, of *joy*, describing the moment when Sisyphus breathes deep and begins his descent, following the rock to which he's eternally bound: "All Sisyphus' silent joy is contained therein."

Camus finds for the defense—against suicide—arguing that death is the only fated fact of our days, that other than death, "everything, joy or happiness, is liberty." To choose our own (living) destiny, he says, no matter how difficult or painful, is a sustaining freedom.

In his diaries, Pavese argues for the prosecution: "To choose a hardship for ourselves is our only defense against that hardship . . . That is how we can disarm the power of suffering, make it our own creation, our own choice; submit to it. A justification for suicide." The writers deploy the same logic but come to opposing conclusions—almost as if their debate were less a matter of philosophy and reason than of perspective, of shifting moods.

"The divagation or digression is a way to postpone the ending, a proliferation of the internal time of a work, a perpetual attempt to escape—but to escape from what?" asks Calvino in *Six Memos*. "From death, of course."

No more digressions, then. Pavese killed himself in the city of Turin on August 26, 1950, overdosing on barbiturates in a rented room. "I forgive everyone and ask everyone's forgiveness," he wrote in a note left behind. "OK? Don't gossip too much."

The epigraph to *This Business of Living* is taken from Dante's *Inferno*, from the circle of the suicides: "As a green brand that burns at one end / and at the other oozes sap and hisses / with the wind escaping: // so from that broken splint, words and / blood came forth together . . ." But the words end. "I won't write anymore," Pavese writes, the last entry in his diaries, and the sentence haunts me as much as any more eloquent phrasing. This is the fear. This is the threat. Darkness comes in the shape of a white page. *Wrong it is for a man to have again what he once cast off*, the soul says, and

Dante weeps, unspeaking, in the seventh circle—Dante, who began his journey lost in a dark wood, in despair, the trees around him black and bodiless against an unseen sky.

Don't join the club, Z. whispered, his lips to my ear and his arms around me, and I didn't, and I won't. I've made it to the other side of twenty-seven, made it to and past an age that seemed so distant to me then, to and past a danger that seemed, then, like the only one that threatened. I haven't tried to kill myself; I haven't come close. The harm I've done to my body is minor and ordinary: wounds due to recklessness and illness, and a few too many years spent drinking far too much. That indulgence was another attempt at happiness, an attempt to get to the place where stars fell from the sky to burrow under my eyelids, where my body grew weightless. I was good at getting to that place. I was bad at staying there. "Mistakes are always initial," Pavese says, and I'd add: balances are always fine.

But embedded in my obsession with happiness is an obsession with its opposite—or vice versa. "Nothing but an illness makes us aware of the profound workings of our body," writes Pavese. "In the same way we realize those of our mind and spirit when we become unbalanced." How mysterious each seems (happiness, its opposite) when glimpsed from the distance of the other, like towering mountain ranges, one in sun and one in shadow. How tempting to explore, each in their own way.

Most of us enter the field of psychology, if we enter it at all, through therapy: another way to wrest themes and meaning from floating details of scene and character, another attempt to turn suffering into something of use. I've seen a psychiatrist just once, a year after Italy, nine months after the crippling depression that followed, in an attempt to stave off another such season. It—or the lithium prescribed along with it—worked. But I didn't need a kind psychiatrist to craft stories from my life—that was my area of expertise. You object, yes: many narratives can be gleaned from a single set of facts, let alone the feelings, memories, and impressions that frame or obscure them. What if the story I tell myself is simplistic, solipsistic, damaging, wrong?

I'm sure it is. Nonetheless, it's the one that interests me—my simplistic, solipsistic justification for just about everything.

"But then Pavese was a Northern Italian," writes Sontag. "Northern Italy is not the Italy of the foreign dream . . . The place is there, but as the unattainable, the anonymous, the inhuman." I don't visit Turin; I don't wake from my monthslong foreign dream. Turin is an invented city, for me, as unreal as Polo's Chloe, Eutropia, Ersilia, and Esmerelda, as impossible as any of Khan's imaginings. For Pavese, it was real in the way that only home can be, hyper-real, gleamed simultaneously with nostalgia, with love, and with shame. He died in a rented room in that hometown, a displacement that echoes that felt in the body about to be cast off. What was once home is no longer.

Or so I imagine. My Pavese, too, is invented, a city I've never visited and yet I describe its battlements, its harbors, the feel of its wind on my face. *Trading cities*, Calvino calls them, and I would trade with these writers, would engage in a barter of words—but I'm a con artist. I take and take and take, giving nothing back. My (stolen) defense: *Who are we, who is each of us, if not things we have read and imagined?* The men are dead, by their own hands or not, but the books: they're still alive, all around me. The gestures outlast the hands that made them—far from empty, so full they fairly overflow. "I remember I was crossing a square and the thought stopped me dead," Pavese writes in another novel, *The House on the Hill*. "I froze; it was an unexpected joy, a happiness."

CITIES & EYES

"C AN YOU HEAR IT YET?" asks the professor, meaning the music of Leonardo da Vinci's *The Last Supper*. In the darkened classroom, the famous work projected on a screen, he points out the chords played by the painting's dimensions, the measured groupings of the apostles, the vanishing point coinciding with Christ's head. High notes sound in the landscape glimpsed through distant windows, arpeggios in the many gesturing hands. "It's harmonic!" he exclaims. "Can't you hear it?" And we lean forward in the darkness, cock our ears, and can.

Born near the mountainside town of Vinci in 1452, Leonardo came to Florence in his late teens to begin an apprenticeship with Andrea del Verrocchio. In Verrocchio's workshop, the young Leonardo ran errands, ground colors for paints, and learned the accepted techniques of shading and form, assisting on the commissions that came into the shop. Some of Leonardo's earliest surviving work can be found in Verrocchio's 1472 *Baptism of Christ*, to which the younger artist contributed, according to biographer Giorgio Vasari, one of the attending angels and the landscape beyond. The delicacy of the angel's half-turned face, the dreaminess of the landscape—we'll see these qualities again.

"We are aware of landscape as something full of movement," writes Kenneth Clark in *Leonardo da Vinci*, describing this early work: "light moving over the hills, wind stirring the leaves of trees, water flowing and falling in cascades. . ." Can you hear it yet? Amid the bustling cityscape of Renaissance Florence, Leonardo recalled the countryside of his youth, the soft glitter of it like a memory, faint at the edges but imprinted as if in wax. "He thought of air, atmosphere, as an almost palpable mass of particles floating between the eye and the objects it perceives," writes Robert Wallace in *The World of Leonardo*, "a transparent ocean in which all things exist and by which they are bound together."

Leonardo drew obsessively throughout his life, sketching landscapes, faces, figures, and plants. Many of these sketches are extant, providing an incomplete account of what he saw, whether with his eyes open or when they closed. On the back of one such drawing, made during those early years in Florence and survived the five centuries since, the artist scribbled a quick note to himself, a record or a reminder: *I am happy.*

I am happy, scribbling notes in a darkened classroom in this light-filled city: *mimesis, perspective, perfection.* When the professor looks away, Annie and I lean over to write in each other's notebooks, interspersing the dates and names of masterpieces with plans for the evening's dinner or the weekend's travel. "The Renaissance was distinguished by artists working with their minds first," the professor says, "and their hands second." A wedge is driven between artist and craftsman, a gap that will widen in the centuries to come. Artists will begin—not yet, but soon—to sign their work. It will matter, who has made what, and not merely what has been made. "This was the result of an increasing consciousness of individuality," writes John Berger in *Ways of Seeing*, "accompanying an increasing awareness of history."

If an individual mind lay behind the work, another stood before it, looking. Perspective was a Renaissance reinvention, explains the professor, its demands met and perfected by Brunelleschi and Alberti and Masaccio. Masaccio, whose name graces the street I live on in Florence, was the first to put a vanishing point in a painting, paving the way for *The Last Supper*'s arrival two generations later. In my notebook, I sketch clumsy imitations: lines converge and planes form, stick figures frozen upon them. (Annie adds punning phrases in thought bubbles above their featureless heads.) The two-dimensional page aches to be more, straining against its bonds.

"Perspective makes the single eye the center of the visible world," says Berger. "Everything converges on to the eye as to the vanishing point of infinity. The visible world is arranged for the spectator as the universe was once thought to be arranged for God."

Verrocchio's *Baptism of Christ* is on display at the Uffizi in Florence, along with the earliest work attributed to Leonardo, the *Annunciation*. The hands of Mary and the angel upending her world, each raised in greeting, possess the lithe grace that will come to be known as Leonardesque, and the landscape shimmers distinctively. But the young artist hasn't yet tuned his ear to the subtleties of perspective: though his measurements are technically correct, the wrong notes sound in the jutting building behind the Virgin, in her strained relation to the plinth and book from which she reads. No harmonies here. Noting the long resistance by scholars to attribute this and other clumsy works to the young Leonardo, Clark says simply, "We must admit that the early pictures are less good than we should expect them to be."

Other wonders, or their potential, haunt other rooms. Annie drags me down the hall to a gallery in which her beloved Giotto enlivens the solemn gold faces of saints—as if, at last, a joke has cracked the world's stern glare. Emotion was as fresh a discovery as perspective to Renaissance painters, having made its triumphant return to European art in recent centuries. Earlier figures, like the golden emperor and empress in Ravenna, were depicted without expression, impassive and stony as the walls around them. But the Uffizi's many Renaissance masterpieces are flooded with feeling, as if each artist had remembered that his subjects—Jesus, Mary, Magdalene, John—were supposed to be human, or near enough. Angels weep at Christ's crucifixion, and the Virgin swoons in agony. Elsewhere, Leonardo's unfinished St. Jerome is wracked with pain: his face wrenched, his hand reaching toward some color yet to come. Grief has entered the hallowed frames of painting, as have rage and ecstasy and even, eventually, less vaunted emotions like merriment and delight. By the High Renaissance, Leonardo's St. Anne beams; his St. John the Baptist smirks; his childlike Benois Madonna is glimpsed midlaugh. How strange it seems, to imagine Mary simply happy—and yet, she must have been. We each have been, at least a moment, and sometimes I wonder if that shouldn't be sufficient: a moment of happiness, scribbled and recalled, enough for one life.

Though I know I visited the Uffizi—how could I not?—I don't remember standing before Leonardo's *Annunciation* or his unfinished *Adoration of the Magi*. I remember the massive golden background of a painting—one of Giotto's?—and Annie's effusive love for it, though I can't make out what she said, not through the muffled surface of so many years. I can picture Botticelli's seaborne goddess huge against a white wall, but is that memory or compilation, the imprint of an image familiar not because I stood before the original (*center of the visible world*) but because I've spent a lifetime in the company of copies? "The uniqueness of every painting was once part of the uniqueness of the place where it resided," writes Berger, but now we're likely to have seen *The Birth of Venus* a few dozen or few hundred times before we visit the original, if we do. "It is no longer what its image shows that strikes one as unique," says Berger. "Its first meaning is no longer to be found in what it says, but in what it is." What it is—that is, the *real* thing.

We'll come back to this.

Real, too, was that afternoon at the Uffizi, a fact defended by the evidence of my notebook: a ticket stub, a matching date, notes on Botticelli's *Columns of Apelles—everything stands for everything else, unending—*and Giotto's *Madonna and Child—these figures have* weight, *breasts and knees.* "That's me," Annie says, having read the sentence above, calling me from across the country to which we long ago returned. "I definitely would have ranted at you about the weight of Giotto's figures."

But I can hardly bring these images to mind, and my own notes feel like a secondary source, written by another. I don't trust them, checking their claims against textbooks, encyclopedias, and the museum's holdings listed online, against Annie's memories of the same places, the same days, her own self of a decade ago. If the past is another country, the past self is a stranger in it. Shouldn't I be the only source I need? *I've seen it with my own eyes*, we say, a claim for veracity, but how can I be sure what I've seen is real? There are so many copies. There are so many of me.

Leonardo left Florence in 1482, entering the patronage of Ludovico Sforza, Duke of Milan. Between crafting costumes, masks, and tableaux for lavish court festivities, he began two massive undertakings: a gargantuan sculpture of Sforza's father on horseback, for which only a model was completed and only a few sketched studies remain; and a painting of Christ and his disciples taking a meal, made for the refectory wall at Santa Maria delle Grazie.

"The thing was born with a birth defect," says the professor, exasperated. Leonardo didn't want to be constrained by the demands of traditional fresco, in which paint is applied to wet plaster, requiring the artist to work quickly and without revision. Instead, he applied a base of his own invention to the wall and worked upon it in tempera. "This disregard for media of execution marked all his most important works," says Clark, a disregard "which sprang not only from impatience and experimentalism but from a certain romantic unreality."

Or, as the professor sighs: "They just don't last." The flawed experimentation of *The Last Supper* became apparent almost immediately: the wall—which backed the monastery's kitchen—was damp, and moisture seeped into the painting. Leonardo completed the work around 1497, and by 1517, Clark writes, observers noted that it had already "begun to perish." When Vasari saw the painting in 1556, he deemed it "so badly handled that there is nothing visible except a muddle of blots." Clumsy attempts at restoration further damaged *The Last Supper* in the sixteenth and seventeenth centuries, and Napoleon's soldiers threw stones at what remained of the masterpiece when they invaded Milan in the eighteenth. So worthless did the work seem that at some point the monks of Santa Maria delle Grazie, in the interest of enlarging a door, removed a huge section from the bottom of the painting, cutting off the feet of Christ.

We leave Florence for Milan, Annie and I, retracing Leonardo's journey in the company of our art history class. We walk the parapets of the Gothic cathedral and visit Sforza Castle to see Michelangelo's *Rondanini Pietà*, his last and unfinished sculpture. The intertwined figures are of the same alien race as the *Captives* in l'Accademia, half-formed: a leg rendered with anatomical precision but only rough stone where a torso should be. Though every book I'll later read considers the sculpture a traditional Pietà, a depiction of Mary holding her dead son, I write down another theory—perhaps it belongs to the professor? To the guide? The finished leg of the figure holding Christ is exposed: no long robe, no modest dress. That bare leg doesn't belong to the Virgin, I write, but to Magdalene—Magdalene, who reached out to touch Jesus after his resurrection and was forbidden. *Do not touch me,* Jesus said, an edge rising in the air between them—a lack, a want—but Michelangelo lets her touch him one last time. With the statue left undone, the bodies of the woman and her savior merge in places, indistinguishable, human and divine hewn from and held within a single block of stone. Their touch is utter, entire, complete—if only because the piece itself was never completed.

"In principle a work of art has always been reproducible," writes Walter Benjamin in "The Work of Art in the Age of Mechanical Reproduction." "Manmade artifacts could always be imitated by men." Indeed, it's common practice for students to copy the work of masters, and early copies of *The Last Supper* provide us with information about the original that might otherwise be lost in the mess made by restorers: Leonardo painted St. Peter's head in foreshortening, for example, St. Andrew's in profile, and Judas as almost entirely turned away from the viewer. Yet even these copies, despite their age and pedigree, remain reproductions, as essentially *other*, as essentially *not*, as any attempt you or I might make.

"In spite of the depressing insistence of these facts," Clark writes of the damage suffered by *The Last Supper*, "some magic of the original remains, and gives the tragic ruin in Santa Maria delle Grazie a quality lacking in the dark smooth copies of Leonardo's pupils. Luminosity, the feeling for atmosphere . . . the fresco, perhaps from its very vagueness, has kept a certain atmospheric quality."

Clark's use of the word—*vagueness*—recalls a parenthetical aside in Calvino's *Six Memos*: "Italian is, I believe, the only language in which the word for 'vague' (*vago*) also means charming, attractive; having originally meant 'wandering,' it still carries with it a feeling of movement and mutability, which in Italian suggests not only uncertainty and indeterminacy but also grace and pleasure."

What better definition for the Leonardesque? *A feeling of movement and mutability, uncertainty and indeterminacy, grace and pleasure.* In the hundreds of drawings that have survived, each pen stroke fairly dances, possessed of a nimble elegance. His figures always seem on the verge of speaking; you can hear bees buzz around his sketched flowers. Leonardo was obsessed with the movements of water and wind, and his style steals from these elements, liquid and airy. (His rival Michelangelo, meanwhile, is all fire and earth.) Mutability is in-built, his grace without question, and yet it's that third quality, uncertainty—our English meaning of "vague," so often meant critically—that seems most vital here.

In a drawing from about 1512, the faint traces of a meadow swirl around a woman's feet; her simple dress falls like the frothy tops of waves. She faces the viewer but her body turns to the left, ready to follow her own pointing finger, gesturing toward something we cannot see. "This should be Leonardo's last drawing," writes Clark, "just as *The Tempest* should be Shakespeare's last play." The woman embodies both Leonardo's aim and his inspiration, her soul on full display in the twist of her limbs and her loveliness laced with something uncanny, something unknown. This sense of mystery, Clark says, is symbolized throughout the artist's work by "the pointing finger and the smile—the one indicating a power outside our field of vision, the other reflecting an inner process which is equally beyond our comprehension."

Mystery within, mystery without—isn't this all art is after, in the end? To illuminate, if not the solution to such mysteries, the contours of their unsolvable forms? All day, the unmeasured world surrounds us, a confluence of forces spanning lightyears and eons and allowing, in this place and time, the sight of sun through the leaves, the fat bees floating by, the hollow-boned birds going wild in the throes of morning. All day, our minds churn away: this naming, this wonderment. "Seeing comes before words," Berger says, the first sentence in his book. "It is seeing which establishes our place in the surrounding world; we explain that world with words, but words can never undo the fact that we are surrounded by it. The relation between what we see and what we know is never settled." The seen and the unseen, the known and the unknown, questions and answers and questions again—they trade places in an endless dance.

And the best artists, the Leonardos, manage to capture some of their steps in ink and oil, unsettled and unsettling. Art began and continued, Benjamin says, in service of ritual, whether magical or religious. Eventually—during the Renaissance, that is—the "secular cult of beauty" took over, and art itself became the god whom artists competed to praise. (Though for some, such as Michelangelo, the God of the Church still spurred an equal will to work.) Leonardo was an acolyte of this secular beauty, voracious in his worship. Nature, fable, anatomy, architecture—everything that interested him (and what didn't?) held mysteries within, mysteries he could approach through math or color or scribbled note.

"It is a high-risk proposition, as Sokrates saw quite clearly, to reach for the difference between known and unknown," writes Anne Carson. "He thought the risk worthwhile, because he was in love with the wooing itself. And who is not?"

But I've gotten off-track—followed a pointing finger right off the page. We were speaking of Benjamin, who says that works of art have always been reproducible, and yet: "Even the most perfect reproduction of a work of art is lacking in one element: its presence in time and space, its unique existence at the place where it happens to be." *The Last Supper* happens to be in the refectory of Santa Maria delle Grazie, on a wall at one end of the large room where the monks who lived and worshipped there took their meals. Leonardo eschewed the pillars and adornments of previous iterations and ignored the strictures of more historical renderings: the setting of his supper is wholly contemporary. The tablecloth, plates, and bowls are of a kind the monks themselves might have used. "Christ was to celebrate his last supper," writes Johann Wolfgang von Goethe in his essay on the painting, "among the Dominicans, at Milan." So simple are the place settings and so skillfully done the perspective that I can imagine one of those monks—glancing up, having forgotten the work recently done by the famous painter—believing, however briefly, that he and his brothers have been joined by thirteen more. In Leonardo's hands, the picture became an extension of the actual room or, as Robert Wallace says, "the actual room became an extension of the picture."

Reproductions can't capture this architectural element, nor temporal ones. "This unique existence of the work of art determined the history to which it was subject throughout the time of its existence," Benjamin continues. "This includes the changes which it may have suffered in physical condition over the years." What an understatement, when the work at hand is *The Last Supper* and the changes it may have suffered include the stones of Napoleon's soldiers and the bombs of World War II. Missing flakes of paint—so incredibly many of them—are evident even in photographs the size of an art book's pages, and no restorer, however skilled, can replace the section cut away. Reproductions and original alike are flawed descendants of whatever masterpiece Leonardo completed in 1497, a work we've never seen and never will.

But only the original was touched by Leonardo's hands; only the original has endured that *unique existence*. This is not mere sentiment, nor fetish for authenticity (though the art world is certainly chock-full of the latter, and this writer inclined to the former).

Paintings live, as we do, in four dimensions, and to equate the centuries-long heft of one with any of its thinner imitators is an incomplete and facile argument. "Original paintings are silent and still in a sense that information never is," says Berger, ". . . [I]n the original the silence and stillness permeate the actual material, the paint, in which one follows the traces of the painter's immediate gestures. This has the effect of closing the distance in time between the painting of the picture and one's own act of looking at it." It is remarkable—so let's remark on it—that the work survived and survives, as familiar to me as a family photograph, as sketchy and as sure as my own memories.

The many reproductions of *The Last Supper* make it feasible for anyone, anywhere, to hear the harmonies produced by Leonardo's brush, and yet those reproductions also impede the would-be student of the painting. Familiarity breeds not contempt but catatonia. "How can we criticize a work which we have all known from childhood?" asks Clark. "We have come to regard Leonardo's *Last Supper* more as a work of nature than a work of man, and we no more think of questioning its shape than we should question the shape of the British Isles on the map. Before such a picture the difficulty is not so much to analyze our feelings as to have any feelings at all."

There it is, one of the fears of approaching an artwork long loved from afar—its origin story obsessed over, everything written about it read—which is also one of the fears of travel, and one of the fears of life: it will disappoint. The work or place or year will not live up to our expectations, or we will not live up to it. We will be thoughtless or fearful or simply not in our right minds. We will find ourselves dulled and distracted. "Numbing," Clark says, of the painting's renown, and what a strange impulse it is: to worry, in the face of something longed for, that we'll be suddenly unable to feel. That the thing desired, like the beloved seen through the clarifying haze of eros, will be no match, in the end, for the desire itself.

•

In Milan's Pinacoteca de Brera, I linger at Cima's *St. Peter Martyr*, the disciple depicted as living with a knife balanced across the top of his head, blade down—"Don't we all," drawls the professor—and Sodoma's *Christ Scourged*. We see Jesus close-up in this painting, just his head and chest, hands bound across it. Framed by shadowy guards, he wears his crown of thorns on the way to his execution, blood trickling from his forehead and tears from his eyes. I've seen hundreds (it feels like thousands) of Christs in the last six weeks, and he is easily, wrenchingly, the most human.

Later, I'll learn that a few of Sodoma's works have been mistaken for Leonardo's over the years, and I'll wonder if this painting is one, with its perfectly molded hands and striking chiaroscuro. And what if it were? Thought to be by Leonardo—or actually by him? "To be sure, at the time of its origin a medieval picture of the Madonna could not yet be said to be 'authentic,'" writes Benjamin. "It became 'authentic' only during the succeeding centuries and perhaps most strikingly so during the last one." How wildly the idea of authenticity swings between two poles: a thing deeply felt, some core or definition, and a thing imposed from without by unfeeling experts at a great distance in space or time. The work has been authenticated, we say, a clinical word and a contradictory one, those poles of meaning clashing in its staccato syllables.

Regardless, the fact remains: were it not by Sodoma, Sodoma's Christ might be the destination of our day's travel, and not merely a stop along the way.

"We never look at just one thing; we are always looking at the relation between things and ourselves," says Berger. "Our vision is continually active, continually moving, continually holding things in a circle around itself, constituting what is present to us as we are." Benjamin and Berger write from a future even an optic-obsessed mind like Leonardo's didn't imagine—at least, he didn't jot or sketch it down—a future where any artwork can be replicated, not in painstaking and imperfect copies made by later and lesser artists, but in the effortless mimesis of photography and film. The perspective deployed by Leonardo and described by Berger—"Every drawing or painting that used perspective proposed to the spectator that he was the unique center of the world"—is necessarily foregone by photographers. "The camera—" writes Berger, "and more particularly the movie camera—demonstrated that there was no center." Any photograph can be taken a hundred ways; any scene can be shot a thousand times, from a thousand angles.

Photography and film take perspective's claim of veracity one massive step further, no detail lost between the eye that sees and the hand that snaps the shutter or taps the smartphone. But the illusion of fealty produced by a camera is just that: an illusion. The photograph's edges are no more arbitrary than the painting's, but, in the world of the painting, nothing exists beyond the frame. If we engage in Leonardo's *paragone*, the act of comparing the arts, fiction provides the written equivalent to painting: the entire truth of the novel is contained, obliquely or not, in its pages. If the author says a fictional wall is blue, it's blue, and no reader can argue otherwise; the book's reality brooks no competition. Not so with photography—nor with nonfiction, its literary counterpart: the world exists, with its billions of viewpoints, beyond the photo and the page. Liberties can be taken and arguments made, and authenticity's baggage grows weightier.

How to carry that load? (You know, I suppose, that I'm not talking about photography or film any longer.) "The painter maintains in his work a natural distance from reality," writes Benjamin, while "the cameraman penetrates deeply into its web. There is a tremendous difference between the pictures they obtain. That of the painter is a total one, that of the cameraman consists of multiple fragments." Here are mine—*these fragments I have shored against my ruins*—multiple and multiplying, section upon section and page upon page. If only I can gather enough of them, piece them together. If only I can restore the picture, ever closer to the original, and keep the paint from flaking, the water from seeping through.

Santa Maria delle Grazie is a small church, no cathedral, with windows set deeply into its brick structure. We skirt its walls to find the former refectory, where a banner above a simple door assures us: the *Cenacolo Vinciano* lies within. The professor distributes tickets as we enter. We are here to see Leonardo's famous painting for ourselves, after so many hours spent with its imitators in the classroom. *In the flesh*, we say of such meetings, meaning my flesh—the work of art has none—but my own physical presence is hardly the miracle, here. The building we enter has been rebuilt entirely since the bombs of World War II destroyed it—destroyed all but one sandbagged wall, that is, which used to back the monastery kitchen. We hand our tickets to a docent and wait for the group ahead of us to finish: only a dozen people or so are allowed into the huge room at any given time. When our turn comes, we walk down a long hallway, glass doors at either end sealing it shut. The docent says something about the air, about filtering and regulation, an attempt to stave off any further damage even at the molecular level—and then we pass through the second door and into the room.

We tend to use the word *aura* loosely, with an intentional vagueness (*vago*), but Benjamin deploys the term with precision, equating it to the "uniqueness" of an artwork. In a footnote, he elaborates: "The essentially distant object is the unapproachable one." Aura, in Benjamin's formulation, is possessed by the image that remains "distant, however close it may be." I think of Carson's would-be lovers, separated by the fine edge of eros; of Magdalene's hand lifting toward the risen Christ, met only by empty air; of jellyfish in a sparkling sea, their otherworldliness within arm's reach. I think of those words—*within arm's reach*—and how the arm in question never does, quite, reach. The shimmering possibility— that it could—is definitional.

The room at Santa Maria delle Grazie seems to me all possibility, nothing squandered. The filtered air, cool and dry, has such substance after the smoggy throng of Milan that I can feel its weight, however faint, against my skin. This still wind fairly billows at my back, filling the empty hall as I turn to face the figures seated along one wall, caught midmeal. They are massive: not giants like the *David* but humans built at a bigger scale, just different enough to unsettle and just large enough to awe. I approach them like an altar, getting close enough that the cluster of saints before me—Bartholomew, Andrew, James the Younger—fills my field of vision. The residue of brushstrokes before my eyes and the air soft along my cheeks, I grip the plush velvet rope placed so as to separate viewer from artwork—*do not touch me*—a distance of just a few feet. Distant, however close it may be, and almost, almost within arm's reach. The docent speaks from somewhere to my right, reciting facts and probabilities I've already memorized and barely register. You understand: How could I possibly hear her, over the music of Leonardo's painting?

"It is the motion of the hands," says Goethe, the hands that distinguish Leonardo's greatest work, such gestures a "resource . . . obvious to an Italian." In other pages, the Italian Marco Polo has grown fluent in the language of the Great Khan, able to describe every detail of the places he has visited, and yet: "[W]hen Polo began to talk about how life must be in those places, day after day, evening after evening, words failed him, and little by little, he went back to relying on gestures," writes Calvino, "holding up his hands, palms out, or backs, or sideways, in straight or oblique movements, spasmodic or slow."

This gesticulation is innate, embedded in our (human, not Italian) circuitry: just as specialized neurons in our brains interpret facial expressions, reading sorrow or joy or deceit in them, others have evolved to interpret the movements of hands, a holdover from the preverbal communication of our distant ancestors. We can read each other's *gesti* like so many skimmed pages. "It is the most literary of all great pictures," says Clark of *The Last Supper*, recognizing the full sentences written in the disciples' uplifted hands.

But Clark argues that our focus on the fingers might stem from the fact that the saints' faces—where our brains' dancing neurons might otherwise find the emotions they seek—have been so badly damaged over the centuries: their visages bear the brunt of past restorers' ineptitude. "Had the original heads been there, with all their pathos and dramatic intensity, the gestures," he writes, could have resumed "a subsidiary role." Instead, we rely on the hands to tell the story. Under such weight, says Clark, their weakness is revealed. "The whole force of gesture, as an expression of emotion, lies in its spontaneity," he writes, "and the gestures in *The Last Supper* are not spontaneous." No, they are not. Among Leonardo's notes, we find these descriptions: "Another twisting the fingers of his hands, turns with stern brows to his companions. Another with his hands spread shows the palms, and shrugs his shoulders up to his ears, making a mouth of astonishment." And another, and another. A good painter must paint both man and the intention of his soul, remember? Our hands most readily hold those intentions, and give them away.

But I find in Leonardo's hands, in Polo's sign language, in Z.'s ready gestures—a constant of these weeks and months—a turning away not from the face's expression but from the words that would pour forth from it. "There is something indecent in words," says one of Cesare Pavese's narrators. "Sometimes I wished I were more ashamed of using them." (I read this line aloud to Z., who tosses one hand up and out in agreement.) Should I be more ashamed—or wish to be—of these thousands upon thousands of words? "There is no language without deceit," says Calvino, or one of his characters, but the revelations of another city argue yet another side: "Falsehood is never in words; it is in things."

An alternative is at work in the body's expressions, both facial and gestural—the pointing finger and the smile. In movements subtle and broad, calculated and spontaneous, an uncrossable distance is hinted at: the distance between one mind and another, perhaps. "In fact, neither reader nor writer nor lover achieves such consummation," says Carson. "The words we read and the words we write never say exactly what we mean." But I must admit, selfish as I am, that the distance I find most unbearable is the gulf within my own mind. I can't articulate these feelings, these mysteries, even to myself. My own language deceives me, full of falsehoods, and I can't shape any of it to my satisfaction.

Language has its limits: this is not a new thought, nor a rare one. But I think those limits are often unapproached, unseen in the flat light of so many days. Life, too, has its limits, and my mind spends most of its time well within the borders of the said and the sayable. Only on the clearest days, the brightest—what I have come to think of as the happiest—does it veer toward and across those edges, does it teeter over the chasms my lines would love to fill. The mystery is glimpsed, however briefly, in the sublime expanse of a seascape or the simple lines of a sketched figure, and this is where I feel language's lack most keenly, where my hands lift from the page or the keyboard, fingers fluttering back and forth in their search, where my face turns as if toward an answer. My whole body becomes a gesture, out here, where words fail.

•

"Now do you not see that the eye embraces the beauty of the whole world?" asks Leonardo, in the pages upon pages of observation and treatise later compiled (by others) into books. "Owing to the eye," the great painter writes, "the soul is content to stay in its bodily prison." Empiricist and artist, voracious and perennially distracted, Leonardo gathers fragments to him with such force and genius that their inherent incompleteness might almost be forgotten. The *whole* world, he says, and I think he means it: the mystery within, the mystery without. One of the pleasures of Leonardo—that is, of his artwork, his writings, his incorrigible experimentalism, his brilliant but flighty mind—is how expansive this world of his feels, *all possibility*.

A certain romantic unreality, Clark calls Leonardo's tendency to shrug off any limiting factor: Why wouldn't unsolvable mysteries seem solvable to him? His engagement with the world is incomparable and unflagging. Where I worry the frayed edges of memory, he praises it: "Wrongfully do men lament the flight of time, accusing it of being too swift, and not perceiving that its period is sufficient. But good memory wherewith nature has endowed us causes everything long past to seem present." Where I despair at the scrim that can fall between me and these words, this table, the suffocating covers of a depressive's bed—even between me and my own brighter, sharper, often inaccessible mind—Leonardo might simply, delightedly, take the scrim's measurements, noting its color and texture and just how it falls.

My Leonardo is just another copy, of course, unforgivably distant from the original and lacking its aura, its authenticity. Or, as Berger says, "The past is never there waiting to be discovered, to be recognized for exactly what it is. History always constitutes the relation between a present and its past." That relation can span five centuries or a decade, can be bowdlerized or scavenging or simply wishful. The left-handed Leonardo wrote his notes backward (from right to left, each letter reversed)—they're most easily read with the help of a mirror. We see through such a glass, darkly or not, attempting to glimpse into times other than our own.

Into places, too. "Elsewhere is a negative mirror," Polo says to Khan. "The traveler recognizes the little that is his, discovering the much he has not had and will never have." In this book full of elsewhere and elsewhen, packed with the words of foreigners and the dead, Italy is edged and lensed, a mirror-country to the real thing. I keep trying, like Alice before the looking glass, to peer around the frame.

The city of Valdrada was built on the shores of a lake: every house and street, every room and hallway doubled in the water's reflection. "Nothing exists or happens in the one Valdrada that the other Valdrada does not repeat," Calvino writes. "Valdrada's inhabitants know that each of their actions is, at once, that action and its mirror-image."

Annie and I abandon our class again at the train station in Milan. "Switzerland is *right* there," she'd said, waving a map at me a few days before, so to Switzerland we go. ("I'll get to Switzerland next week," I'd protested, mildly—we have a week off from classes coming up, and I've been poring over the timetables that came with my Eurail pass—but Annie ignored me, rightly, and booked a hostel.) We take the train across the border to Lugano, an Italian-speaking city set against the southern foothills of the Alps and built on the shores of a lake with which it shares a name. It's dark by the time we arrive, and we walk the small city's marble, almost-carless streets graced in the soft glimmer of lamps tucked into doorways. We are giddy from the long day and unbearably silly, making jokes about armies, neutrality, hot cocoa, and cheese. Bundled up at an outdoor table aglow from the restaurant's nearby windows, we insist on a dinner of beer and chocolate, local delicacies. You'll forgive us the mess of our joy, spilling over—mere hours ago, you see, we'd been in another country. It's nearing the end of October and still, still we can eat outside.

The next day, we take a funicular up one of the mountain's slopes, make another meal of beer and sheer delight. We lean over old stone walls, professing our love for Lugano to the huge mirror of the lake and the Alps beyond. The air is crisper at this wooded height, bright and brown and autumnal, as if the season has reached this far, and no farther. We race it back down. The sun shines in the sky above and the lake below, every bit of the day doubled. In those twenty gleaming hours, my only desire—my only want—is for the time to continue. And isn't that incredible? To live, however briefly, a life so good one only wants it to go on?

Between diagrams for flying machines and instructions for young artists, between notes on the way blood pumps through the human body and the sketched faces of saints—turning to their Lord in dis-belief, their fingers leaping in shock and sorrow—Leonardo writes in his backward script:

> Behold the hope and the desire of going back to one's country . . . of the man who with perpet-ual longing looks forward with joy to each new spring and to each new summer, and to the new months and the new years, deeming that the things he longs for are too slow in coming; and he does not perceive that he is longing for his own destruction. But . . . I would have you know that this same longing is that quintessence inherent in nature, and that man is a type of the world.

Perhaps the mystery of this longing didn't feel solvable or even articulable in Italy, but livable—right in front of my eyes, and myself content to look. Within arm's reach was close enough, no need to grasp: for answers, for words, for more. *The traveler recognizes the little that is his, discovering the much he has not had and will never have.* A kind of comfort, that—for who would want to have everything? What would I long for, then? It's a moot point, when it comes to the mysteries hinted at in Leonardo's sylvan figure, in his backward notes, in the silent faces and lilting fingers of his damaged saints: I'm in no danger of solving them. My words can only form a gesture, a finger pointing beyond the page.

CITIES & NAMES

L EAVING THERE AND PROCEEDING toward the east, the traveler arrives in Budapest, a city of gleaming bridges and turreted, white-stone buildings that catch and echo the sun's rays so that the source of light in this light-filled city seems to be multifarious and without end. Set along a broad and gentle river, the two hills of the city rise on either bank, and if what one seeks doesn't exist in one half, surely it can be found in the other. From the near side, full of ancient monuments and tree-lined parks, the traveler can look across the glass-clear river to the beckoning glint of museums and shops; from the bustling swell of that far side, the traveler can admire the stately rise of the other's wooded landscape, its foliage gilded in a dozen shades of gold. The special quality of Budapest, for the traveler arriving on a morning at the end of October, stepping from the stale air of the overnight train into a soft breeze, is how the city seems, between its two equally lovely halves, to contain every wonder one might wish to glimpse: the oil paintings of ancient masters; children tossing bread to birds in a dappled pond; the old stone shoulders of castles where kings and queens once ordered the building of roads and universities and libraries great enough to rival those of distant empires, long since destroyed.

But the true beauty of Budapest lies in how the traveler, certain that she will find what she seeks within its pristine squares and watery light, feels no urgency to begin her search. She is content to linger at a table set with gold-rimmed plates in an immaculate café atop a hill, the city's highest point, where she looks through windows twice her height at the sky, the river, and the city in which all that she desires awaits her, ready—when she is—to be claimed.

On the train, a tiny old man babbles extravagantly in an unknown language, blowing thankful kisses at his fellow traveler, who stoops to retrieve the gentleman's thin-rimmed glasses from where they have fallen in the aisle.

Traveling farther to the east, the visitor to Bucharest notices first the hunched shoulders of each building, the screams of graffiti scrawled across their pockmarked faces, the scaffold-thin ribs of the dogs who roam in packs near the city's center. When the traveler catches a child slipping his hand into the pocket of her unbuttoned coat, she swears at him in a language neither of them speak. But the young pickpockets of Bucharest, like the buildings, merely shrug.

Every second façade in the central square hides behind a pillar of scaffolding, but no workmen clamber upon them: the city of Bucharest persists in a constant state of change, ever attempting to escape its past and never quite gathering the right tools, the right time, to shear the scowls from its buildings. The traveler ducks under metal crossbars to enter a museum where she is the only visitor—as if it were a museum made for her, she wants to think, and can't. This place wasn't made for anyone. In its many empty rooms the statues proclaim victory, yet each has lost its head. A series of frames holds sketches for a falling figure—the whole, the legs, the left arm, two renderings of the same plummeting thumb—though where the finished work might be, no docent can say. The city's god is depicted over and over, yet never completely: paint peels from tempera-on-wood, leaving only an eye here, a robe there, a hand upraised to bless or condemn.

Leaving the museum, the traveler buttons her coat against the cold. Ducking under the sagging wooden planks of another construction site, she enters a café where she can contribute to the smoggy pall of the city, smoking behind closed windows. The plates are gold-edged and the lamps glimmer in the room's many mirrors, but the gray sky through the window, through the smoke, dims the light of each. The visitor to Bucharest sees the city only through a veil—the city prefers it that way.

On the train, a stranger shares the traveler's compartment, reaching across the seats to nudge her shoulder, over and over, insisting upon something in a language she does not want to know. His eyes are feral and his breath dark, and the traveler does not sleep until the sun rises and her fellow traveler has disembarked.

Entering Vienna for the first time, the visitor recognizes its broad streets, its spired government buildings, its great gray cathedral and distant Ferris wheel, its statues and gardens. Rare is the traveler who sees Vienna with surprise, for the city is its own chief export, its elegance repeated and magnified a thousand times in literature, film, and music. Walking its squares at dusk, lights coming on in the windows, the visitor to Vienna experiences the uncanny sensation of being a character in a favorite movie, or finds herself walking, unconsciously, to the strains of a beloved song. These things were made in Vienna but have traveled so far, for so long, that the traveler associates them with her own memories, with cities she has known more intimately.

In this way, Vienna—this model city, this city to which other cities aspire—is a place of dislocation, ever shifting. Its incomparable beauty becomes familiar, and the welcoming smiles of its broad façades grow unctuous. The traveler finds herself unsettled, unable to appreciate the delicate masterpieces in each museum or a street performer's handsome grin, for at every turn she feels the vast and growing gap between the real Vienna, beautiful as it is, and the Vienna she has known from a distance, a city full of romance and adventure, of insight and dreams, of the swelling triumph of symphonies underscoring (she had thought) every step. But her steps are accompanied only by their own soft fall, so light that she might miss the sound were she not listening for it, straining toward any reassurance that she does, in fact, exist.

The visitor to Vienna ducks down every side street in search of something she has not seen before, some moment worthy of capture in script or song. She finds only trim cafés, soft lamps coming on beside tall and untouchable doors, and, hidden at the distant end of a lovely square, a museum filled with nothing but clocks: astrolabes and sundials; pocket watches in the shapes of flowers, busts, and violins; grandfather clocks taller than any living man; wooden contraptions too large for their cases, set directly on the floor. They resemble nothing so much as the machinery found on farms, and their purpose would be utterly mysterious, were they discovered anywhere else. Here, their purpose—if not their means of achieving it—is evident. In this temple to the gods of horology, room after room hold only those inventions made to track their makers' passing through.

On the train, the traveler rests her head against everything she has and sleeps.

•

The ancients built Zurich at the head of a long lake, at the foot of towering mountains. The wealth of centuries, like water flowing down from the snowmelt in spring, has accumulated here. Proud buildings gleam along the most important avenues, and shops sell objects of fine-spun gold, of stainless steel backings and pearl inlay, of silk and emeralds. But the most precious commodity offered by the city is not one that can be carried away by any traveling merchant or wealthy customer. Zurich, alone among the great cities of the region, possesses and is possessed by an impenetrable silence. The vehicles traveling its streets make only the faintest of noises; its inhabitants lower their voices to be heard. The visitor to Zurich, strolling those avenues or entering those shops (the doors on muffled hinges, no jangling bells), can never be sure whether this silence lies within or without, a product of her inability to master any of the city's many languages or a thing imposed upon her, a faint wind in her ears. Walking the promenade that skirts the lake's southernmost edge, the traveler is startled by a tumult of birds rising from the water's surface, their bodies white against the gray. Their movement is so sudden, a burst of wildness against a clockwork backdrop, that it takes a moment before the traveler realizes: it is not the unexpected motion of the birds that has grasped her attention, but their careless and deep-throated cries.

On the train, hours slip one into the next unnoticed. Lives come and go a hundred times before every disembarking. Forgetting the lateness of each particular hour, the traveler glances out the window, anticipating landscape. But night has always fallen, and she finds only her own estranged reflection in the glass.

•

The first sights the traveler to Copenhagen sees are the spires that rise amid the colorful tumult of buildings, each as enchanting as a fairy tale. One is striped in bright greens and yellows like a carnival tent, spreading; another is spun of fine, filigreed gold that sparkles in the light; a third billows in the city's wind like a dancer's skirt; the metals of another, pale and dark, twist around each other like ice cream in a child's cone; another holds windows and balustrades, this highest part of the structure below a structure unto itself. And yet these spires disappear as one approaches, ducking behind less-decorated edifices. No matter how intently the traveler keeps her eyes fixed on them, how carefully she calculates the angles made by the streets and parks and harbor, she cannot match the pinnacles above with the buildings below. The traveler, glimpsing a particularly lovely spire to the east, walks toward it, eager to see what place possesses such a tower, but just as she thinks she must be there, nearly there, she searches the sky to find that the spire is behind her, glittering in the blueness to the west. The spires of Copenhagen form a second Copenhagen above the first and more familiar, a city unto itself, unreachable by any stair.

The visitor to Copenhagen, however, is not frustrated by the fruitlessness of her search nor by the labyrinthine shifting of the city's skyline. How could she be? For there is the sparkling harbor, there the dancing shadows of seabirds along the pier, there the hearty shouts of fishermen and the fine blue wind casting its invisible nets through the salty air. No, Copenhagen is an ideal city, possessing both kinds of beauty. (There are two.) There is the beauty at hand—harbor, seabirds, shouts, wind—and there is the untouchable beauty of the spires, always out of reach. Rather than competing, these beauties sustain each other: without the elusive upper city, the loveliness of the lower would grow dulled and banal; without the reassuring charm of the ground, the mystery of the spires would become unbearable, and the traveler thwarted and bitter. Instead, she is alternately sustained and uplifted by Copenhagen, city of comfort and adventure, where a great loveliness surrounds her and an even greater loveliness waits to be found.

On the train, a young woman has lost her ticket, or her money, or never had the money for a ticket in the first place—the traveler doesn't speak the language and can't be sure. When the old woman sitting beside her leans over, handing her own money to the conductor, every occupant of the car smiles in benevolent witness.

Berlin is not a single city but split into two: one broad and one towering, one bright and one gray, one of steel and one of stone, one of rivers and one of trees. The sun rises upon the monuments of one and sets over the shops of the other; in one, the last days of fall cling to bright leaves, while winter picks its way through the other's bare streets and abandoned plazas. Seasons, days, citizens, facts: all are demarcated by the division, each object or memory native to one side and foreign to the other. A truth in one Berlin is always a lie in the other.

Naturally, the inhabitants of each city believe it is *they* who live in the real Berlin; the other—which they know of, but never visit—is the imposter. Like two halves of a severed brain, the Berlins cannot know how close they lie to one another, nor how small a spark might bridge the distance. They remain defined by their differences: one waking and one asleep, one narrow and one splayed, one decked in reds and one in yellows, one burnished and one translucent.

The visitor to Berlin has heard of these two cities, yet no matter how far she wanders nor how closely she looks, neither can be found. Seeking the wall that divides them, she finds only rubble; seeking histories and directions, she finds only lowered voices, turning away.

•

On the train, countries pass in a matter of minutes, are devoured by the afternoons. Some landscapes are scoured in the long, golden mornings; others pass unnoticed in the dark. Shaken awake by border police, the traveler offers her passport in lieu of language. Money in lieu of language in the café car, smiles in lieu of language when she meets the eyes of her fellow travelers. She grows mute, her own useless language swallowed down into the deepest part of her, compressed and fit to bursting. On the train, her only conversations are with the days.

It is easy to become lost in Prague: streets twist at unexpected angles, doubling back on themselves or veering sharply away; dark houses cling to the cobblestones, crowding out the sky above; the hills themselves seem to shift with the day's shadows; the river disappears under fog. A square that seems familiar is edged by buildings never seen before, as if the city, which has played a hundred roles throughout its history, is still trying on various masks, seeing which one might fit. Walking these steeply curving streets, the traveler gets the sense that the very stones of the city are shifting under her feet, that they might give way to chasms or cliffs. The cathedrals and castles roofed in green and gold might turn, at any moment, into ramparts of black and steel; the shops proffering jewelry and scarves might sell only knives and cigars; each flowering garden and park might slip the scrim it wears to reveal a graveyard. This is the legacy and the dark-hued pride of Prague: its citizens know their city is but one of many that stand on this very spot, just as the world they live in is but one possible world. They know the impossible lies but an inch below or behind or alongside the visible, and the traveler to Prague—catching her foot on a step that wasn't there, she is certain, a moment ago—the traveler knows it too.

•

On the train, her only conversations are with the days. But the traveler imagines she might some day tell another of the cities she has seen, might recount the scaffolds and the silence and the spires and the clocks. She might lay her words at another's feet and watch them rise, forming buildings and bridges, rivers and hills, streets she might wander down once more, turning a corner as lightly as a page.

Everywhere the traveler turns lies water. The city of Amsterdam shines like glass in the sunlight, in the dusk, in the gleam of streetlights after dark. Since the city was built on the banks of a great river centuries ago, that river has multiplied as if an ancestor: its descendants course alongside every street, stamping the city in a watery grid, full of curvature and tangents. One cannot walk without walking along water, or over it. Canals form concentric half-circles like some interrupted rings of hell—but Amsterdam is no inferno. Bridges of simple stone complement the scrubbed cheeks of old houses, and markets overflow with books and flowers. The visitor to Amsterdam is offered choices as plentiful as the merchandise of those stalls: the quiet bar or the bustling café, the grand palace or the sprawling fairgrounds, the museum dedicated to one great master or the museum dedicated to another. The visitor can enter either; the visitor can enter both. Many lives can be lived in Amsterdam, city of reflection, where each stream branches only to converge again. The sky seems to stretch a little more broadly here, a few feet below sea level, and cars and boats and bicycles are lined neatly along each street, as if one could travel anywhere and any way one wants.

But where might that be? The visitor to Amsterdam wanders its shining streets, stands before the paintings of its great masters, buys its books and flowers, and knows nothing more can be asked of a city than this: both possibility and its fulfillment. If the traveler feels any lack, it is not the city's fault. The city is riverine, offering a thousand routes and ways, and if the traveler cannot build a bridge or steer a boat to span them, the flaw lies not in this city's brick or wood or stone but in the other city, the other, the one she carries on her shoulders.

CITIES & THE DEAD

W E HAVE A WEEK OFF from school and I spend it alone, crisscrossing the continent on overnight trains, visiting eight cities in ten days. I feel like a far less glamorous Polo, sleeping upright in my seat and subsisting on dining car coffee, a ragged backpack tucked beneath my feet. I gather no wondrous objects or glittering trinkets but only photographs, the cities distilled. I take pictures of old walls and tall doorways, of billboards and birds, shops and ponds and monuments—I find Goethe in Vienna, Kierkegaard in Copenhagen, Kafka in Prague. I carry Gilbert's poems and Pavese's diaries with me, my only interlocutors.

"Traveling is a brutality," Pavese writes. "It forces you to trust strangers and to lose sight of all that familiar comfort of home and friends. You are constantly off balance. Nothing is yours except the essential things—air, sleep, dreams, the sea, the sky—all things tending toward the eternal or what we imagine of it." Nothing is mine, not even my name, left behind with Annie and Vig and Z.; not even my language, these words by which I define myself forsworn. Nothing is mine except Pavese's essential things, and this fact devastates at times, at times uplifts. For the first time in two months, *home* becomes an alluring concept, though I'm not sure where it is. The trees of Hungary and Germany begin to turn outside the train's window, pretty as the woods I grew up near, an ocean away. But returning to Florence—exhausted, exhilarated— offers a new kind of joy, another aspect of the happiness of simply being there.

The trees of Florence, too, have begun to turn, but we break out our coats and continue to wander the city most afternoons. Annie and Vig and Z. and I walk from the school to the bar, from the museums to the bookstores. We walk along and across the Arno to take pictures from the top of San Miniato, to throw darts in a bar at its foot. We go to dinner at a restaurant south of the river where we're seated upstairs, a room all to ourselves. A piano stands in the corner, and Z. plays its shining keys until our server arrives, admonishing. Wandering afterward, we stop before the huge window of a glassblower's studio, staring at the fragile translations of light behind the pane. The artist sees us and invites us in. He and Z. talk shop while I pet the glassblower's dog, a small, curly-haired creature whose dark eyes shine as if crafted by his master. The artist shows us the kiln, the vermiculites, and Z. tells me how glass beads must be heated and cooled, heated and cooled again. I take this tale of treasure, another metaphor for madness to add to my collection.

And once or twice or a hundred times, walking home in the misting night, I climb, light with wine, to walk along the broad walls that line the river. The warm streetlamps of the city blossom on one side, as if within reach of my outstretched fingers, and the frigid Arno whispers on the other, gliding blackly below my boots. What a delight, to wear my happiness so easily, to walk along a self-made precipice and choose with every echoing step not to fall. Z. extends an arm in my wake, holding his hand just behind my knees as I go and keeping it there until it's time to come down, until we reach the street that leads away from the river, away from the night, toward the glowing lights of the city's center and our temporary homes.

We take the train to Rome, where the Tiber glistens in the muddy November sun and living people laugh amid the buildings of the dead. We begin at the beginning, or near enough, spending our first day in the city with some of its oldest structures. The ruins of the Forum stand against the Renaissance and Baroque and neoclassical architecture of later centuries, surrounded by the signs of modern times, captured—as much as they can be—by our fervent cameras. I want to say: The past is present, here; or, The past lingers, loitering on every street corner; or, Here, the past is just another stunning landscape, as staggering and pervasive.

But it isn't the past that strikes me as an interloper, but the present: the apartment buildings and cars and cameras seem as strange as UFOs would, landing amid the properly ancient ruins of the Forum. (Or as unsettling, in their way, as the anachronisms that begin to appear in the later pages of *Invisible Cities*: airports, antennas, refrigerators, radios, and Ferris wheels fill the cities described by Marco Polo, who traveled in the thirteenth century.) In Rome, it's the people who don't seem to belong in this city from another century, and another, and another—it has outlived so many—and I feel as out of place as any time traveler, as amazed at my own arrival.

We tend to use *history* and *the past* synonymously, though they're not the same. Both are nouns, but we might think of *history* as an adjective or adverb, descriptive and relational; history doesn't overlap with the past but points the way to it, an indication or qualification. The past is a thing unto itself, and history is but one way (among many) we can relate to it. In his essay collection, *Sometimes an Art,* historian Bernard Bailyn includes a definition of history as "the critical, skeptical, empirical source-bound reconstruction of past events, circumstances, and people." In other words, history is manmade. The past is not.

But Bailyn adds a delightful final amendment to this definition: such source-bound reconstruction must be "based on the belief that the past is not only distant from us but also different." I like the gentle nod of *belief,* as if the essential difference of the past might be disputed. Yet it helps to be reminded, once in a while: the people who walked through the Forum when its columns and arches were new—their minds fired by the same complex processes as mine, and the same starry universe grew around them, but it's hard to overstate the unknowability of just about everything in between. Their world smelled different, tasted different. Historians, Bailyn says, in their consideration of those big, world-changing events by which we abbreviate the past—Pompeii, the Sacking of Rome, Augustus and Caesar and crossing the Rubicon—shouldn't forget the small facts that filled the air around that past's inhabitants. Such was the stuff of their life: the smell of waste; the absence of machinery's noise; the constant, ordinary threat of death at forty or thirty or twenty or less.

These aspects of the past can be kept at the edge of the mind, if never embedded in its center. We can't know them like we know the scents and sounds and fears of our own everyday. But we can catch them in the corners of our eyes, can approach as a horizon. Perhaps, as Calvino says in *Six Memos,* "the true work consists not in its definitive form but in the series of attempts to reach that form." Perhaps the historian is another one of Zeno's travelers, shearing away at another unending distance.

That distance grows, of course, with every day: the past expands like the universe. History grows along with it, every new approach layered atop the paths tracked by earlier societies and their scholars. What is distant history to us—the Renaissance, say—had its own distant histories; even in the past, the past loomed. When a young, already-renowned Michelangelo Buonarroti arrived in Rome in 1496, the city's obsession with its own ancient history was in full swing. Pope Julius II, who would become the artist's most demanding patron, was an ardent collector of recently recovered antiquities like the *Apollo Belvedere* and *Laocoön and His Sons*. The latter was discovered in 1506, half-buried in a vineyard, and Michelangelo was among those who witnessed its extraction from the earth. Julius rewarded the discoverers of the *Laocoön* so richly, writes Robert Coughlan in *The World of Michelangelo*, that he "inflamed the already hot search for buried masterpieces" and "Rome became pockmarked with diggings."

The past lies not behind but below, its treasures there for the taking. "Every era cannibalizes the previous one," writes Anthony Doerr in *Four Seasons in Rome*. The bronze of one masterful sculpture is melted down to make another; the stones of the Colosseum are quarried to build St. Peter's. "Meet the new temples," says Doerr, "same as the old temples." Built and rebuilt, made and remade, Rome has scavenged its own past for its present glory for more than two millennia. Today, the city continues to sink as surely as Venice, not under water but under the dirt and trash and architecture of the continually renewing present; ancient Rome lies deep beneath our feet. This fact reminds me of Calvino's Argia, a city which "has earth instead of air." (The activities—or inactivity—of Argia's inhabitants are unknown.) "If you average it out over the millennia, the detritus has piled up over Rome at somewhere near an inch a year," writes Doerr. "Hadrian would have entered the Pantheon by *climbing* stairs. Now we have to brake the stroller as we coast down toward it."

So Rome comes to resemble a palimpsest: each civilization is scraped away and replaced with the next, but something remains, able to be glimpsed beneath the thick ink of today—whenever *today* might be. The historian's task grows close to the archaeology it's always resembled, if only in metaphor: "the world we know," writes Bailyn, contains, "however deeply buried, the residues of those past worlds." And we tear at the earth to get to them: our books, our minds, our lives, pockmarked with diggings.

We visit the Vatican, where Michelangelo stood atop scaffolding most days for four years to paint the Sistine Chapel's ceiling. The project was a bugbear to the young artist: at thirty-three, he considered himself a sculptor (*David* and the *Pietà* behind him) and thought the demands of the massive space were beyond his capacity, then unproven, as a painter. He thought—perhaps rightly—that his enemies were behind the commission, rooting for him to fail. But the ceiling was what Julius demanded, so to the ceiling Michelangelo lifted his brush.

You know the most famous panel: God afloat in that brain-shaped swirl of cloak and angels and Eve; Adam grounded on a rocky outcrop, reclined but reaching. The inch of air that separates their fingers is one more uncrossable edge, electrified with want and promise. *They touch not touching*, as Anne Carson says. *Conjoined they are held apart.*

But eight other panels span the ceiling's expanse, a dozen smaller scenes border them, and sibyls, prophets, *putti*, and *ignudi* fill every interstitial space. The ceiling above is as crowded as the floor below, where I crane my gaze upward in imitation of the painter and try not to bump into other tourists, their eyes similarly occupied. Though lofted as high as any cathedral, the frescoes seem to hang low over the space, the many muted colors of the paint lending weight to the surface, heavy and dense.

The vague unease I felt in the cave at Capri returns. Again, surely, the fault lies not with the place but with me: some inner flaw, drawn to the surface. An inherent dissatisfaction, perhaps, or a temperamental resistance to any beauty I can't swallow and feel within. Or perhaps I just expect too much of these famous, distant places, expect them to hold the happiness I've traveled all this way to find, and hand it over. How could they possibly meet these expectations? The thing desired will never be a match for the desire itself, remember?

Though it was—in the dining room in Milan, on the cliffs of Cinque Terre. The boundless world has lived up to my boundless longing for it, and this, too, I ought to remember.

In the Sistine Chapel, all I want—inexplicably, greedily—is for the thing to be *bigger*.

"History is the subject of a structure whose site is not homogenous, empty time, but time filled by the presence of the now," writes Walter Benjamin in "Theses on the Philosophy of History." In other (lesser) words, it takes a conscious resistance not to impose our own concerns onto our ancestors, not to paint them from the very particular angle of our own time and mindset, inescapable conditions that they are. This resistance may well be impossible, though Bailyn and his fellow professionals aspire otherwise: "As historians we shrink from telescoping past and present," he writes, "hoping to explain the things that happened for their own sakes and in their own terms."

It won't surprise you to know I make no such attempt in this history, minor and personal as it is. I write from a distance of eight and nine and ten years, and the time I write about—a particular autumn in a particular place—is filled by the presence of Benjamin's *now*, which is to say: my now, which shifts by the minute but comprises a series of different seasons spent far from Italy in more ways than one. But I try, sometimes, to brush it from my eyes. "The past is a different world," says Bailyn, "and we seek to understand it as it actually was." Yes—I want to understand my past as it was, if only so it might be preserved or recreated. Amateur that I am, I'm attempting a *source-bound reconstruction*, trying to codify and verify the very days I lived. Why? Why isn't it enough to have lived them, to recall their contours without interrogation?

"Reflection shows us that our image of happiness is thoroughly colored by the time to which the course of our own existence has assigned us," writes Benjamin. When you're looking for happiness, I've found, you see evidence of it everywhere, the broken branches or faint hoof prints left by an animal long-tracked. (Though these signs mean only that the beast *was* there, and is no longer.) My eye leaps to *happiness* on any given page—even here, in this essay by Benjamin that has little to do with eudaimonia and much to do with war and the threat of Fascism and the inescapable (if so often avoided) brutality of both history and its present iteration. How to be happy, in the face of such things? We can't, we can't, and yet we are. So much is buried, and we—I—neglect to dig. I'm "a spoiled loafer in the garden of knowledge," as Friedrich Nietzsche said, as Benjamin quotes, as I take and flee with, back to the pretense of *homogenous, empty time*, as if I might outrun the context of the words, their history.

I'm reading Giovanni Boccaccio's *The Decameron* for my class on Italian literature. Traditionally, the British professor explains, stories operate on a scale in which the positive value is morality— the reader roots for the heroic good guy and against the nefarious bad. Not so with *The Decameron*, she says. Boccaccio's positive value is intelligence: a character's cleverness redeems her from any moral failing. Other qualities dominate other books: in *Wuthering Heights*, for example, passion is the governing mode. Heathcliff and Catherine are our touchstones as readers, not because they're morally better than Edward and Isabella—they're certainly not— but because they're more exciting. *Positive values—*, I write in my notebook, hurriedly and without a doubt, *mine is happiness.*

Italy's is beauty. From the Greeks, the Romans took (along with plenty else) *kalokagathia*, the idea of beauty as moral, the two qualities—*kalos* (beautiful) and *agathos* (virtuous)—intertwined in a single word. What is lovely is good, what is good is lovely. The word originally served as a standard to which men should aspire, a loftier equivalent of our *chivalry*. In my copy of Aristotle, it's translated as *gentlemanliness*, just as *eudaimonia* is reduced to *happiness*, each word shedding a skin of meaning as it slithers into another language.

The idea emerged in early Christianity (and, elsewhere, in early Islam) as an architectural influence, the reason for the grandeur of churches like those in Ravenna. It coursed through the work of the anonymous monks of the Middle Ages, transcribing and illuminating manuscripts as a form of prayer: by making the pages beautiful, they aimed to strengthen their belief. And it flourished in the Renaissance, when artists awash in Neoplatonism crafted sculptures, paintings, and cathedrals that held the divinity they hoped, after death, to touch. "My eyes that ever long for lovely things," begins a poem by Michelangelo, "My soul that seeks salvation, cannot rise / To heaven unless they fix their gaze / On beauty, for they have no other wings."

"This art will someday be perfected," said Leon Battista Alberti of the work of his fifteenth-century contemporaries. Alberti was a mathematician as well as an architect, artist, and writer, and math was one more method of perfection for artists who believed everything *could* be perfected, from sculptures to souls. "So was I born as my own model first," writes Michelangelo, "The model of myself; later would I / Be made more perfect." Why not? It must have seemed possible in that time, in that place, in that rush of art and intellect, the whole continent manic and remade. Doesn't it still? *She's perfect*, Vig says in a hostel in Capri, watching Monica Bellucci's lips fill our television screen. Beauty—a perfect, archetypal beauty—is the great Italian export and enduring positive value; *bella* is hollered on every block. You'd think the word would devolve, spindling into meaninglessness, but there are the cathedrals, there the museums and piazzas, there the Arno and the Adriatic, spilling light. *Che bello*, we say, every day, everywhere, half-joking—imitating our host parents, exaggerating our accents—but we mean it, too. *How beautiful.*

Days come when Kublai Khan has no patience for the elaborate reports of Marco Polo, when the emperor retreats within his robe of silk and gems, disgruntled and disbelieving. Khan snarls at the explorer before him: "Your cities do not exist. Perhaps they have never existed. It is sure they will never exist again. Why do you amuse yourself with consolatory fables? I know well that my empire is rotting like a corpse in a swamp . . . Why do you not speak to me of this? Why do you lie to the emperor of the Tartars, foreigner?"

Polo obliges the emperor's dim view, conciliatory: "This is the aim of my explorations: examining the traces of happiness"—my eyes fly to the word—"still to be glimpsed, I gauge its short supply. If you want to know how much darkness there is around you, you must sharpen your eyes, peering at the faint lights in the distance."

This art will someday be perfected, said Alberti, and it was—wasn't it? *The Last Supper*, the Sistine Chapel, these pinnacles of the High Renaissance: they were painted within a few decades of Alberti's death. But perfection is the prerogative of the future or the past: the present is too porous to hold it. "Nobody has the whole of it," reads a fragment of Michelangelo's, echoing Aristotle, "before he reaches the limit of his art and his life." The obsessions of the era's artists seem to be evenly split: here lies the grandeur of the classical past, tugged from the earth below, and there the promise of the flawless future, a vision glimpsed by looking upward—to an altarpiece, ceiling, or skyline. (Call the former memory, maybe; call the latter desire.) The dominant faith of the Italian Renaissance was similarly torn, equal parts tradition-bound Catholicism and an unwavering belief in that future, in the perfectibility of the world in which they lived, not just the next one. Remember the early, unsuccessful planners of Florence's Duomo, faced with the problem of the dome: *They merely expressed a touching faith that at some point in the future, God might provide a solution.*

"The fact—the inescapable fact—is that we know how it all came out, and they did not," writes Bailyn of the past's inhabitants. "The natural orientation of their experience was to their past. Our perspective, in studying their lives, is formed by what proved to be their future, which is our past, the ignorance of which was the most profound circumstance of their lives."

Michelangelo didn't want to paint the Sistine ceiling. His best chance at perfection, he thought, lay elsewhere. Julius had commissioned him to design and sculpt his pontifical tomb, a monument grand and massive enough to echo the mountains from which its marble came. The artist's earliest plans, in 1505, called for a freestanding structure over thirty-six feet in height, adorned on every side with statues—at least forty in all—and containing a chapel in which the pope's body would lie, a pharaoh of old entombed in his pyramid.

But such a majestic creation required an equally majestic locale. The perfect setting for his final resting place, Julius decided, would be the rebuilt basilica of St. Peter's, a project not yet begun. The Pope turned his attention to St. Peter's, and handed Michelangelo the Sistine commission in the meantime. When Julius died in 1513, his tomb was incomplete—was, in fact, barely underway. Michelangelo was forced to modify his grand plans, reducing the freestanding structure to a more modest wall monument; by 1516, the plans called for a mere façade. The demands of a new Pope (and another) interrupted Michelangelo's work again (and again), and the tomb wouldn't be completed until 1545, forty years after the original plans were drawn. Forty statues had been cut to seven, the location downgraded from St. Peter's to San Pietro in Vincoli, and—though the thing bears the dead pope's name—Julius's heirs didn't bother to move his remains. The tomb isn't a tomb at all but a cenotaph, an absence of bones below.

How far from ideal (or Ideal) this must have felt to ambitious, fervid, perfectionist Michelangelo. (Another poem of his begins: "I cannot but fall short in mind and art . . ." Teaching these poems, the literature professor jokes: "If Michelangelo were alive today, they would have given him some Prozac and he never would've produced anything.") How unhappy must have become this happy-making thing, the act of working. Perfection seems possible only when we're engrossed in our work, wholly and happily lost in the middle of things, shearing away at a block of marble or sketching an arch's curve—but that possibility disappears with distance. How many times Michelangelo had to step away from this once-desired project, how thoroughly he must have known its imperfections. And yet he kept at it, because of contract or reputation or stubbornness or some improbable hope eternally springing.

Did he know he'd already rendered the artwork that would make him so immortal as to seem divine, not in marble but in paint? But he hated working on that infernal ceiling, shoulders aching and paint dripping in his eyes. The Sistine Chapel's adornment is a true fresco, painted in swift sections upon wet plaster laid fresh each day, the work measurable in these *giornate*. The art demanded as much of the artist's body as of his mind, and Michelangelo didn't seem to relish this added challenge, this physical manifestation of his spiritual striving. ("I've got a goiter from this job I'm in," begins a poem written at this time.) If he didn't see any chance at perfection in the painting while it consumed his days, how could he have grasped its greatness afterward? Can looking back ever prompt a vision of one's work better—not truer but more light-filled, more transcendent—than that glimpsed from within? I have my doubts. But whether he knew it, then or ever, the fact remains: the great artist's most famous work was one he didn't want to make. The Sistine Chapel—the First Day of Creation, the Sacrifice of Noah, the Creation of Adam—was a consolation prize, a failure.

We know how it all came out, and they did not.

We go to dinner in Rome, Vig and Z. and I—Annie is taking a private tour of the Sistine Chapel with the other art history students. "They let us lie down on the benches," she'll tell me later. "It was *amazing*." I can't or won't spend the money, wary of my own unease and how easily it finds me, even here. I eat and drink instead, perfect pasta and red wine on white tablecloths. Vig leaves to meet up with other friends, and Z. and I smoke alone on the Spanish Steps, fending off the flower-sellers who mistake us—his arm stretched along the step behind me—for a couple. *Bella*, the flower-sellers say, that catchall word, *bella*, and I don't know whether they mean me or the roses they press into my open hand. *No*, Z. shakes his head, when they look to him for payment. *No, grazie*, I say, handing the roses back, and if the words are tinged with hurt, well, the pain is tiny and exquisite, clenched like a gem. The fountains of the city sparkle; the lamps on their posts sparkle; the night air fairly gleams. I lean back to exhale, and the cigarette smoke plumes against the dark, starless sky like a brushstroke. ("Too much beauty, too much input[;]" Doerr writes of Rome, "if you're not careful, you can overdose.") We wander the lamplit streets, a little lost, until we find the Trevi Fountain—another monument decades in the making—and linger before the luminous water, though we don't throw any coins. I am too proud to make my wishes known, to make it known that I wish for anything.

•

If history is one way we approach the past, memory is another. Memory is different from critical, researched, source-obsessed history, Bailyn writes: "Its relation to the past is an embrace." So why can't I simply open my arms? Perhaps I have and yet, something keeps slipping through them. History, memory: Which one am I after, after all? Which is truer? Which brings the past, both recent and distant, more fully to life—or to life's finest imitation, however pale? Each method feels simultaneously insufficient and overwhelming: too much information, too many conflicting accounts, more details than anyone could possibly hold and know—and yet, it all adds up to something *less*, less than the slightest trace of the thing itself.

There's something productive in this grasping, though—isn't there? They're not mutually exclusive—history, memory—and I'll take any approach I can. Does my best hope lie in bringing them together, two halves of a knucklebone? How else to explain the piles of books around me, the histories and essays and poetry and a fictional account of imagined conversations between an explorer and an emperor who were, in fact, real people, who lived for so many years and have been dead for so many more? Art is one more way we grasp at the past, the dead. For forty years, Michelangelo turned and returned to statues commissioned by a man long gone, to a structure built to guard the air around his bones. There's disappointment in the result, yes, an absence or a less-ness—but the *Captives* emerged from that absence, and so did the *Moses*, horned and flowing and sublime. Michelangelo thought this latter sculpture the most lifelike he had made, and what a gift that is: to have made something, anything, remotely like life.

Khan shakes off his despair and grows exuberant, convinced of the beauty, rightness, and perfection of his lands—"made of the stuff of

crystals"—and he becomes impatient with Polo's circular account-
ings, his ledger of shadows and doubts. "Why do you linger over
inessential melancholies?" Khan asks, and Polo insists that he is
merely making way for the greatness of the empire yet to come,
for a city that will outshine all the others. "When you know at last
the residue of unhappiness for which no precious stone can com-
pensate," the explorer says, "you will be able to calculate the exact
number of carats toward which that final diamond must strive." I'm
pulled up short, finding my favorite word buried in its opposite,
and stumble over the impenetrable surface of the metaphor. Polo
is saying something about balance, something about measurement,
but I, like Khan, feel only extremely and all at once.

"Leave home, leave the country, leave the familiar," writes Doerr.
"Only then can routine experience—buying bread, eating vegetables, even saying hello—become new all over again." Remember
Pavese's diary entry: *The only joy in the world is to begin.* Here lies
another possible explanation for my happiness, this sustained and
sustaining newness: it's November, after all, and still each ordinary
day—each breakfast, each cigarette—is tinged with cinematic light.

In Rome, we visit the Pantheon, leaning back on our heels to
resist the road's downward slope. Built under Hadrian's rule in the
second century, the Pantheon was the largest dome in the world
for centuries, until the completion of Florence's Duomo; it remains
the largest of its kind—concrete, unreinforced—today. The largest, the loveliest, the most brilliant, the most holy: so many pinnacles occurred here and then, the here and now is overcast with their
long shadows. Rome had already earned its nickname—the Eternal
City—in the first century B.C. (And so far, so good, where eternity
is concerned.) The newness felt by me or Doerr or any visitor is a
projection of our own fresh arrival; the ancient place has little to do
with it. And wouldn't Rome or Florence or Italy entire, given more

time, grow familiar, as anything lived with long enough? Isn't it a blessing—how short these months, how finite? Aren't I an idiot, for wanting them to go on?

It's as contradictory as eros, this want: to continue to begin. We enter the Pantheon, where sunshine pours through the oculus in a single column, solid as dirt and striking as diamonds. The routine—light, literal occurrence of every day—becomes new all over again. The thick, vertical ray of sunlight makes this indoor space seem a work of nature, vertiginous as a cliff face, and I think of the word *sublime*, in the old Romantic sense: a thing edgeless and uncontained, *tending toward the eternal*. Though it is in fact the bounded nature of the light that staggers me, the unnaturally stark delineation of its edges. Perhaps its sublimity lies in the improbability of those edges and the threat of their sudden erasure. Shouldn't they burst like a dam, so weighty the flood of particles pushing against them? But they don't.

"A taste for the sublime is a greed like any other," says the writer Annie Dillard, and I am greedy beyond belief. But the sublime—like its Italian cousin *terribilità*, a word used to describe the work (and the character) of Michelangelo—is hardly a sustainable route to happiness. Inherent is some element of startle or expanse or threat withheld, some opening, widening, beginning. The failures of history, memory, and art are as uncountable as their achievements, but I'm especially saddened by this one: that no later effort can recreate (impossible word) a moment of first encounter—and that remembering such a moment can, in fact, erase it. As Sarah Sentilles writes in *Draw Your Weapons*:

> Scientists used to think memories were stored in
> the brain like files . . . You need a file, you click
> on it, and it appears, intact, complete. But they
> now know memory doesn't work like that: you
> don't find your memories; you make them. Every

> time you remember something, you create the
> memory again, strengthen it, build it up, change
> it. The act of remembering alters the memory
> itself. The more often you remember something,
> the less accurate it becomes.

I wonder if history doesn't work this way, too, despite the best intentions of historians—every paper and book shaping and refining a past that never was. And if whatever I'm attempting here (here being now, my hands on these keys, miles and years from Italy)—whether history or memory or some other method of grasping at my own vanished past—must necessarily diminish the force of that past, chipping away at precisely the unnamable, insistent quality that compels this writing. With each attempt to get closer to the heart of this happiness, am I being pulled away instead, inch by inch and word by word? Perhaps I'm the poorest possible caretaker of these memories, which have been entrusted to no one else, found nowhere else in this widening world. I spend them as carelessly as days. I find myself thinking of the smashed toes of the *David*, of the mad urge to hack the sublime into pieces small enough to carry in our pockets. But what else can we do, when the best method of preservation would mean leaving the fruit to rot and stink?

The election has just occurred, back in the States, and we pass a billboard that shows the handsome, smiling face of our next president, captioned with the exuberant headline: IL MONDO CAMBIA. The world changes. I feel a flush of love for my own, abandoned country, a place whose founders deemed happiness so essential they declared the pursuit thereof to be an inalienable right. In fact, the word—happiness—appears twice in that famous paragraph ("[I]t is the Right of the People . . . to institute new Government, laying its foundation on such principles and organizing its powers in such form, as to them shall seem most likely to effect their Safety and Happiness"), a distinction unearned by life or liberty.

Only pursuit was promised, of course, not happiness itself—not even the God of my country's founders could make that guarantee. And the word meant something different than it does today: the prosperity or well-being or sense of purpose implied by eudaimonia would have clung, still, to the English translation. Their word is loftier than the one I'm trying to elevate, befitting a great document; it wouldn't have struck them as incongruously as it does us, its meaning having shifted with the centuries.

Still, they could have stuck with property, and didn't.

Michelangelo returned to the Sistine Chapel in 1536, commissioned by a new pope to paint the towering wall above the altar. (Julius's tomb, again, would have to wait.) While the ceiling is composed of discrete scenes, ordered and arranged around architectural flourishes, *The Last Judgment* depicts an uninterrupted swirl of chaos. Souls rise to heaven and plummet to hell; angels and demons soar and torment; and the Christ who stands amid this frenzy, directing its spiritual traffic, is a monstrous behemoth, all nightmare and no dream. Gone are the idealized figures of *David* and the *Pietà* and even the ceiling—Michelangelo had grown disenchanted, writes Coughlan, with the Neoplatonic beliefs of his younger days. The Ideal—to be sought in "the good, the true, and the beautiful"—was a fantasy; beauty—once a means to enlightenment, as well as goodness—was shunted aside, shorn from the edges of his *terribilità*. Only the terror remained. The Christ of *The Last Judgment* is more raging and unapproachable than his Old Testament Father; the God above, separating light from the darkness and earth from the seas, grows meek and mild beside him.

It was only in the 1920s that critics spied a self-portrait hidden in the piece. Surrounding Christ is a ring of saints, each proffering evidence of his martyrdom—whether as desperate plea or simple identification, I don't know. Bartholomew—one of the Apostles, last seen on the wall in Milan—holds his own skin, carved from his living body before he was crucified. In that flayed and drooping face, broad and lifeless as a Halloween mask, viewers saw the hollowed eyes of the aging artist; in the skin severed from its body—and not the body itself—they found the self-portrait of a man who'd left none behind. "For the first time," says my literature professor, speaking of Michelangelo and the modernists, "we were capable of looking at a work of such grandeur and seeing the human doubt within it."

"How are we supposed to know these things?" says the art history professor, throwing up his hands. He's speaking of another painting, another theory, but I think of the words constantly and now, staring at the sunken face supposed to be Michelangelo's. "It's just people imagining things." Just people imagining things, but we're always convincing ourselves that our imaginings are real: one more route to the past, the dead. Imagined or real, the identification has clung to *The Last Judgment*. It's too good a story, too neat a metaphor: the artist as a man shorn from his own flesh, only skin where a body used to be. All that agony, offered up like a sacrament. The symbolism suits dramatic, self-loathing Michelangelo, enduring pain both physical and spiritual in the service of his art and his God. Standing in the Vatican, I can't help thinking that all those saints crucified, burned alive, stoned and pierced and blessed with stigmata tell a single story: what is holy hurts one, marks one, makes one good. Beauty wasn't the only route to goodness; suffering would do. "To represent faithfully what is inward, by that which is outward," writes Johann Wolfgang von Goethe, "was the highest and almost only aim of the greatest masters." So this greatest master turned himself inside-out, like Calvino's creature made grotesque: an outside with its inside exposed.

To begin his *Last Judgment*, Michelangelo had to cover several earlier artworks: an altarpiece by Pietro Perugino, two other
paintings, three standing figures, and two lunettes, painted by
Michelangelo himself in the course of his work on the ceiling
thirty years before. "For every image of the past that is not recognized by the present as one of its own concerns," writes Benjamin,
"threatens to disappear irretrievably." This is my favorite vision
of Michelangelo: the old artist working in the room of his youth,
that ceiling like a memory above and behind him. His own, ancient
brushstrokes before him, vanishing under the new. Catching
Adam—that old enemy—in the corner of his eye. Turning away,
and back.

In the distant city of Eusapia, "to make the leap from life to death
less abrupt," says Polo, "the inhabitants have constructed an identical copy of their city, underground. All corpses, dried in such a
way that the skeleton remains sheathed in yellow skin, are carried
down there, to continue their former activities." The city of the
dead is not static but evolves like any other, and its inhabitants are
always making changes to their surroundings. The living citizens
of Eusapia, eager to keep up with their underground counterparts,
have taken to imitation, following the trends and innovations of the
Eusapia below. "They say that this has not just now begun to happen," Polo concludes, ". . . [I]t was the dead who built the upper
Eusapia, in the image of their city."

In the upper Rome, the massive walls of the Colosseum loom
at the Forum's end, its stone cut open in a hundred places to let
through the hordes: tourists, now; spectators, then. The once-white
travertine limestone is thick with gray and black, age running down
its face like a mistake of paint. Begun around 72 AD and completed
eight years later, the amphitheater served as the site of gladiato-
rial combat, animal sacrifice, and execution for four centuries. It's

hard to keep this bloody past in mind, though: we enter the outer arches, walk the open hallway, and step into an arena flooded by a blinding and incongruous sun. (*You walk into the sunlight to make yourself happy*.) Only sky serves as ceiling to the crumbled expanse of terraces and stairs, another sublime rearrangement of light that seems to contain the uncontainable. The Colosseum is vaster than its measurements by far, and I feel myself growing vast within it, briefly—so briefly!—and equally uncontained. It's one of the most beautiful places I've ever seen.

"It's possible to stand on land where great violence has been done and not know it," writes Sentilles. It's also possible to know it, and not to feel it: too ancient, too distant, too–long dead. To know it, and not know what to make of that knowing. Beauty, goodness: one doesn't assume the other, whatever centuries have tried to teach us. Beauty and evil, too, can live in the same stone, the same arches and columns. Beauty can be twined with terror, inseparable and buoying—as in *terribilità*—or the two can simply coexist, indifferent to each other. Not everything is part of some larger, lovelier order. (Besides: Is it possible to stand anywhere else? What inch of this green earth has escaped great violence?)

Our art history professor broadens his topic of study for the occasion, speaking of the place's political history, but I can't reconcile emperors and generals with the stone at my feet, the camera in my hand. I no longer feel history's presence but its absence: if history can be defined, most simply, as a sequence of past events, it's not those events that surround us but what they've left behind, an erasure or photonegative, these walkways and arches sloughed off like so much dead skin. Rome is just a footprint or a gravestone: whatever remains to be seen, far more is missing.

Far more is buried. A hypogeum was built below the wooden floor of the Colosseum, a maze of cells and hallways in which enslaved people and captured animals could be held, waiting to be led out and upward—another kind of Eusapia, this lower layer, this underground city of the dead-to-be. (During the Medieval era, the structure was repurposed as a cemetery, the metaphor made literal.) The Colosseum's floor has deteriorated in the centuries since, and the hypogeum is exposed to our eyes and cameras, though we aren't allowed to walk its crumbling halls. Sunlight falls on moss growing in the broken-open cells. I can't see anything but sky over the amphitheater's ruinous, towering walls, can't see the churches or government buildings I know are there. The ruins live next to the Renaissance, the Baroque, the Fascist and the modern and the buildings just now being raised from their foundations, as if every time might be happening all at once, here—here, where all roads lead.

"I think we are always hunting something that is hidden or merely possible or hypothetical, something whose tracks we follow as we find them on the surface of the ground," writes Calvino in *Six Memos*. There's no doubt about this act of hunting: through history, through memory, through art. But my quarry is a shapeshifter, taking the forms of places and people, sculptures and sky. Even the abstractions of words slip from my grasp: I dig at *happiness* until I reach *eudaimonia*, forsake *joy* for *sublimity*. We are hunting something, Calvino says, *something*, and we founder, failing to name it.

We keep speaking, though. I'm reminded of a hypothesis, proposed by some neuroscientists, that infantile amnesia (our inability to remember anything before a certain age) might be due not to a still-developing brain but to insufficient language faculties—that, though memories are often nonverbal, we might need words to form and keep them. The best history, writes Bailyn, is "both a study and a story," both words stacked like barricades and words strung together, a path around or through or under. Words as embalming fluids, preserving, and words as the shovels with which we dig.

Because my self—my younger self, leaning toward Z. on the

Spanish Steps, holding her breath in the Colosseum—she's as dead as any of them. Isn't she? I can't reach her, can't speak with her, can't quite recall her face as it was, distinct from that captured in photographs. I can glimpse her only dimly, through this scrim of years and words; I'm stranded on the other side, and the distance widens. I—she?—can't act on that past, can't improve or atone or do over.

And I would, I would do everything over. I didn't visit the catacombs, nor the ancient baths, nor the graves of Keats and Shelley. I didn't see Caravaggio's *Crucifixion of St. Peter*, nor the lessened, lacking tomb at San Pietro in Vincoli. Or if I did, I don't remember—and if I don't remember, sole historian of this life that I am, then no one does, then nothing happened.

But I've spent too long before these tombs already. Who knows if they hold the bones they claim? I linger at their inscriptions, and the present races away. *Does your journey take place only in the past?* Khan asked, or imagined asking, Polo. The longing that comes with memory is too easily tangled with regret, confined to the past as it is; confined to the past, it carries no hope of wonder or surprise. The ceiling hangs too low. "The past is not for living in," says John Berger, a warning to time travelers like me. It's time to go, time to leave this city occupied equally by the living and the dead.

CITIES & THE SKY

H ERE, IN THE FLEETING PRESENT, I write in a room walled with light wood, dark brick, and concrete. The furniture is warm, all mahogany and cream. A single floor-to-ceiling window stands in the southwest corner of the room, its view evenly halved between a brick parapet below and the sky above. Sunlight falls through the window in the long opposite of a shadow, shifting from one wall to the other over the course of an afternoon. Often, I find myself leaving the desk and taking a book to this solid block of light, my skin warmed as I stand within it to read.

This room sits on the top floor of a school library, where I've been given an office for a year. The floor is locked to students and rarely entered by librarians; most days, it's just me and the special collections up here. When the office grows too close around me, or when I need some visual middle ground between brick and sky, I walk down the hall and lean out over the library's central atrium: four airy stories of books and light descend to a travertine floor. Huge, perfect circles have been hewn in the concrete of each interior wall, allowing glimpses into the stacks and carrels and windows beyond. Concrete crossbeams, thick as a body and tall as a story, form an X above the space, just beside my downcast head; they're so massive, so weighty, and yet they seem to float. From this vertiginous height, the scents of paper, stone, and sunlight in my nose, I seem to be floating, too.

You could say I missed a place—I do, and I do. Surely, then, the place must have something to do with it. In *The Architecture of Happiness*, Alain de Botton writes, "Belief in the significance of architecture is premised on the notion that we are, for better or for worse, different people in different places—and on the conviction that it is architecture's task to render vivid to us who we might ideally be." Substitute *travel* for *architecture*, and I find a statement equally appealing if, perhaps, equally arguable. Shouldn't the place be an end, not a means? Isn't it horrifically narcissistic to fly thousands of miles only to chronicle the wanderings of my own brain, taking snapshots of sites visible only behind my own eyelids? Finding only—as poets and self-help guides alike tend to say—myself? Even my beloved Cesare Pavese succumbs: "Life is not a search for experience but for ourselves," he writes.

But I didn't *find* myself in Italy; I didn't need to; I wasn't lost. I didn't mind living within this skin and flesh, whoever they belonged to—she would do. What I found was a staggering amount of beauty and story and sublimity; I found a longing so strong and constant it could almost sate itself. It was enough; it was more than enough. Immersed in such a state, thinking and feeling at a higher intensity and greater rate than usual—I understand the impulse to call the self experienced in that moment a truer one, somehow more authentic than our distracted, slovenly, dull, impatient, unexcited, everyday selves.

In his book on my favorite subject (happiness, not architecture, though the latter gains with every page), de Botton argues for the validity of this impulse. He dubs it "a troubling feature of human psychology . . . the way we harbor within us many different selves, not all of which feel equally like 'us,'" and makes the case that our access to those other selves "is, to a humbling extent, determined by the places we happen to be in."

In Paris, then, who am I? The school has organized this trip, led by my art history professor and centered around our Leonardo seminar, though other students—Z. among them—tag along. We visit the Louvre, the one-time home of France's rulers turned, after the Revolution, into the largest museum in the world. Works that once belonged to the monarchy, like the *Mona Lisa*, became national property and were supplemented by the spoils of war: *Laocoön and His Sons* was among the plundered pieces that lived here briefly before returning to Rome after Napoleon's defeat.

Even on a weekday morning in mid-November, the room holding the *Mona Lisa* is too packed to traverse; the professor holds court outside the door and lets us brave the crowds at will. I won't. I'm happy to stand before the lesser-known Leonardos in the hallway: *The Virgin and Child with St. Anne, Virgin of the Rocks*, and *St. John the Baptist*, generally agreed to be the artist's last painting.

"That strange work of his late years," says Robert Wallace, calling the *St. John* "disturbing." And perhaps it is. The Baptist is painted in striking chiaroscuro, his flesh soft and glowing against a nearly black background. His wide eyes meet the viewer's, and he smiles faintly if not fully—an expression called, in every book I've read, *enigmatic*, and often compared to the more famous smile in the next room. His left arm holds a furred skin worn as loosely as a toga, and his right curls upward: shoulder bared, hand foregrounded, and finger, yes, pointing. Not onward but upward, though when I follow it, only the Louvre's ceilings can be glimpsed.

Isolated, mysterious, with no landscape illuminating the canvas behind him—it's an odd depiction of the saint (though it came to be imitated, like all of Leonardo's inimitable work). Elsewhere, John is a beatific child, watching over his divine baby cousin, or a gaunt prophet, proselytizing in the desert. He preaches and baptizes and gets beheaded, Salome dancing in the background. Here, he's wilder than we knew—or, perhaps, just as wild as we've forgotten. He lived on locusts and honey, after all, in the gospels of Mark and Matthew, and though his cheeks are full and his shoulders solid, something starved as an animal lives in those eyes. His smile hints at—I want to say *wickedness*, but let's settle for *mischief*. He shows no sign of piety, bears no symbol of his sainthood other than the thin, reedy cross held in his left arm. This cross is so faint and fine it isn't even visible in some reproductions, including the one in my copy of *The World of Leonardo*. You understand, then, why I tend to forget about it.

His is a voice not crying out but whispering in the wilderness, beckoning the viewer back into the darkness from which he leans. He threatens, confuses, entices. This is the Baptist as Bacchus or Loki—near-feral, ambiguous, sly—transformed like Michelangelo's *David* from the Biblical hero to a pagan god, to someone less heroic and more interesting, to something larger than life. Something *like* life, maybe, as we wish it were or as it could be, at its most sublime: thrilling and menacing all at once. He has no need of symbols; he is one. Returning his gaze, a thorny feeling stirs in the shadowy depths behind him, behind me, as if some totem lives there, some answer to all my questions, if I could only strike a match to see.

Three hundred miles south of Paris is the château where Michel Eyquem de Montaigne spent his last twenty years writing the *Essays* in a tower room. "Having committed himself to what he hoped would be a contemplative new life," writes Sarah Bakewell in *How to Live*, "Montaigne went to great trouble to set it up just

as he wanted it." Windows overlooked a courtyard and the surrounding landscape; murals covered the walls, and quotes from
classical thinkers adorned the exposed beams of the roof; a thousand books—Ovid, Caesar, Plutarch, Seneca—lined a set of shelves
rounded to fit the tower's form. "We need our rooms to align us to
desirable versions of ourselves," says de Botton, "and to keep alive
the important, evanescent sides of us."

It's a paradoxical description—an evanescence kept alive, a
fleetingness suspended, these adjectives sustained until they turn
into nouns—but I find such a quality, paradox or not, in the writings of Montaigne, that best inheritor (says I) of the ancient Greek
philosophers and their quest for eudaimonia. His gleeful tangents;
his ranging, self-debating mind, brimming with contradictions; his
shrug in the direction of conclusion or decree: all conspire to pro-
duce essays that lift and lift and lift and do not fall. "To essay something is to test or taste it, or give it a whirl," says Bakewell, of
Montaigne's name for his chosen form (or its chosen formlessness):
"One seventeenth-century Montaignist defined it as firing a pistol to see if it shoots straight, or trying out a horse to see if it han-
dles well. On the whole, Montaigne discovered that the pistol shot
all over the place and the horse galloped out of control, but this
did not bother him. He was delighted to see his work come out so
unpredictably."

A delight, certainly, to be surprised by one's work. There are
crevasses of the mind still to be stumbled upon, still to be hewn and
widened. And if such happiness can be found in the mind's unexpected depths, then what of the life's? Could this be one route or
definition: to be surprised by our own days? To see them unfold
beyond imaginings we didn't know we had?

I knock lightly on the door of Z.'s hotel room. His roommate—for
this trip, not Vig, not anyone I know—opens it. "I'm his wake-up

call," I say. The roommate shrugs into his coat and leaves, and I enter the half-lit room, its curtains pulled against the morning sun of Paris. Z. looks up at me through half-mast eyes. "Hey," he says, and rises onto one elbow, the sheet falling from his chest. He pats the empty inches of bed beside him, smile twitching to a grin: "Come on in."

"Desire keeps pulling the lover to act and not to act," Anne Carson says, quoting Sophokles.

"Get dressed," I say, laughing and hitting the lights. "We're going to miss the train."

The train goes to Chartres, where the stained glass has lasted for seven centuries, has seen Renaissance, Reformation, and Revolution come and go. The sun has vanished behind a fog-white sky, and the cathedral seems colorless from the outside, the light gray of its stone interrupted only by the darker gray of its windows. Inside, it's a different matter. The nave is shrouded—the gray walls, seen from the dimly lit interior, are almost black—but what little light survives falls blue and red and gold on our faces, hands, the floor. The air is thick with color, and I can only imagine the dense pleasure of a sunny day, how luminous the stained glass of the windows must be in a brighter light. They're a pinnacle of achievement, these windows, the professor tells us, like the sixth-century mosaics of Ravenna or Renaissance frescoes: the technical demands of an art form were met and crested here, a culmination of faith and labor. That they've survived centuries' worth of violence—each piece of glass, like Dante's bones, was removed from the cathedral for safekeeping during World War II—is a beauty, like the light, I find hard to grasp.

A year after our visit, the French Ministry of Culture will begin a restoration project on the cathedral. The project involves painting the building's interior a soft but shining white, an attempt to dissipate the darkness we walked through. Critics of the project will argue that the windows look more striking against the shadows or that gloom suits the Gothic architecture; they'll be overruled. "The people who built this cathedral intended that its interior should be light," Malcolm Miller, a Chartres tour guide for more than fifty years, will say in defense of the project. "There was nothing natural about its darkness."

"This building was conceived as a whole," he'll say, "as a book that people could read."

"When buildings talk," writes de Botton, "it is never with a single voice." A Gothic exterior might belie bright rooms within; a bare Modernist entryway might give way to a lush parlor. These varied forms, de Botton continues, "may testify to unresolved squabbles about the nature of happiness." Unresolved, perhaps because they are unresolvable: despite Aristotle's thorough musings on the subject, no conclusion has stuck in the centuries since. Epicureans, Stoics, Skeptics: each proposed their own route to eudaimonia and definition thereof, building so many different temples to so many different gods. The omnivorous Montaigne embraced the influence of these Hellenistic philosophies and more, quoting at length and at leisure from any thinker he could get his hands on; the *Essays* are studded with the words of others.

But Montaigne rarely speaks of happiness as directly as his predecessors did (or as I might wish, scavenger that I am). In a short essay titled "Of Sadness"—which begins with promise, as Montaigne bluntly declares himself uninclined to the emotion— it soon becomes clear that by *sadness* he means grief: the sorrowful examples he cites are parents who've lost their children (as Montaigne himself did, five times over). In "That Our Happiness Must Not Be Judged Until After Our Death," he takes up the titular proposition found in Aristotle and echoed by Michelangelo. Montaigne quotes Solon: "[T]hat men, however fortune may smile on them, cannot be called happy until they have been seen to spend the last day of their lives"—and yet, I hardly think I'll be too happy after that. In his essay, Montaigne considers happiness as a measure of success, a ledger entered and tallied up, something which might be quantified and its quarrelsome nature resolved.

Of course, this isn't what I'm after. And it isn't what de Botton means when he refers to contradicting architectural aesthetics as "two varieties of happiness." A process, not a product, is our subject; I want the act of building and the life within, not the empty structure. The metamorphosing cities of Calvino offer different varieties of happiness, too, and of unhappiness, madness, fear, and hope. The city of Thekla is perennially under construction, in order "that its destruction cannot begin." Andria was designed and continues to be altered in communion with the shifting stars and planets above. Beersheba's inhabitants aspire to another, greater Beersheba, rumored to hang in the heavens above their heads, and race to distance themselves from a third Beersheba, filthy and sodden below. When cities talk, we might say, it is never with a single voice. They're like us that way.

We leave Chartres and its solemn morning behind for a shining afternoon in Versailles; the sun, as if loyal to the place's long-dead occupants, has peeked its head from the clouds to add to the gleam. Within the palace, chandeliers sprout from every square of ceiling; every dripping bit of gold and crystal is doubled and tripled in the mirrors lining every hall. My own face shines back from a dozen surfaces, inescapable and compromised. In celebration of this excess, or in service to it, several massive chrome sculptures by Jeff Koons have been installed in the one-time home of Marie Antoinette. I'm annoyed by the modern intrusion; Annie is livid. "*Goddamn Jeff Koons*," she groans. Staring up at a bright magenta balloon animal, I agree: "I can see why the peasants revolted."

We escape Koons and Antoinette's ghost and our own reflected selves; long gardens stretch flat and flowerless behind the palace like something out of Lewis Carroll. I'll be reminded of their cold symmetry a few years later, watching Alain Resnais's *Last Year at Marienbad*, that fractured narrative of a foreign romance and conflicting memories. (*Desire is a moment with no way out*, I'll think, as Resnais's hero becomes trapped by a maze of mirrors and doors.) Walking the gardens of Versailles, we might be in such a movie, might play characters more intriguing and more elegant than we are, in our jeans, our new century. It's not groundless, I think, not trivial: this desire de Botton describes, to be elsewhere and therefore other. It isn't foolproof, certainly, but I struggle to find a better method of transformation. Surrounded by beauty, we might be more inclined to aspire to beauty ourselves. "Behind wanting to own the painting and hang it where we could regularly study it," writes de Botton, "might be the hope that through continued exposure to it, its qualities would come to assume a greater hold on us."

Continued exposure—in *How to Live*, Bakewell describes Montaigne's early, obsessive fear of dying. She attributes this to too much study of classical philosophers like Cicero, who declares: "To philosophize is to learn how to die." Bakewell writes, "If you ran through the images of your death often enough, said his favorite sages, the Stoics, it could never catch you by surprise," but this trick didn't work for the young Montaigne. He grew increasingly frightened and anxious instead, until an actual close encounter with death shook the fear from him.

But might the Stoics have the right method, if the wrong focus? Couldn't we adopt their reasoning and apply it elsewhere—to beauty, say, or happiness? Couldn't we keep our minds alert to these better possibilities, constantly seeking them out or imagining them present? Believing I might, at any time, be surprised by happiness—isn't this a kind of happiness itself?

•

The library in which I write—many years after leaving Italy, after leaving Paris—was designed by the architect Louis Kahn and completed in 1972, the year *Invisible Cities* was published. In the periodicals room on the ground floor, a glass case holds two models of the building from Kahn's workshop. Made of plain brown cardboard, one depicts the nearly-cubic exterior of the library, neat and geometric; the other pulls the building apart, exposing those floor-spanning circles. Working in the library holds many pleasures for me, and this is one: to gaze at the rendering of Kahn's vision while I stand within its realization, to look at cardboard walls from which the walls around me rise.

"We know that we can bathe just as well under an 8-foot ceiling as we can under a 150-foot ceiling," says the architect Kahn, "but I believe there's something about a 150-foot ceiling that makes a man a different kind of man." *The notion that we are, for better or for worse, different people in different places.* Some would call this a delusion, another kind of tourist trap or platitude, but I can't argue with the way I feel, leaning over the atrium or walking the sun-dappled stacks; I can't disentangle the memories of my happiness from images of vaulted ceilings, arches and porticos, landscapes framed by windows and the light they shaped. Of course we're different people in different places—we're different people on different days, even, in different hours and minutes. "If I speak diversely of myself, it is because I look diversely upon myself," writes Montaigne. ". . . [T]here is as much difference found between us and ourselves as there is between ourselves and others."

Reading Wendy Lesser's biography of Kahn, *You Say to Brick*, I find one version of myself tucked within its pages, like the model of the building housed in the building itself. "I see the library as a place where the librarian can lay out the books, open especially to selected pages to seduce the reader," says Kahn, relayed by Lesser. "There should be a place with great tables on which the librarian can put the books, and the readers should be able to take the

books and go to the light." There I am, *the reader*, existing both on
the page and in the building, looking up from the sentence—*go to
the light*—and into the light I've unthinkingly entered, the light by
which I read.

"Desire, not necessity, is the motivating force," says Lesser of
the library in which I work: the way its curving, travertine stair-
cases lead me from the ground floor to the airy atrium, the way the
climbing stacks of books guide my gaze up and out of its downcast routine, the way the concrete above my head or under my fingers makes me want to be similarly grounded and yet afloat, solid
and punctured all at once. "Need is so many bananas," Kahn says,
delightfully. "Need is a ham sandwich. But desire is insatiable and
you can never know what it is."

The first snowflakes emerge from a white sky, so fine and pale I
think they're only a trick played by the light or my own eyes, something shaken loose from their corners. It's Sunday, our last day in
Paris, and I sit outside of Notre Dame, where Mass has just let out.
I attended the service while groups of tourists moved through the
aisles surrounding the worshippers sitting in the pews. Their cameras flashed from the dark alcoves even as the priest delivered his
homily, even as he consecrated the bread and wine, and I seethed,
unbelieving though I am, at the way each click and burst of light
made the ancient place seem cheapened, fake.

Now I sit on a marble bench across from the cathedral's towering face, watching more tourists—or perhaps they're worshippers,
how would I know?—trickle out of the great doors into the greater
emptiness of the square. In an essay, "Thinking the City," Calvino
cites a letter from Giacomo Leopardi in which the poet, visiting
Rome, is amazed at "the disproportion between human dimensions
and the size of buildings and spaces." As if our lives might grow
large within them, I thought upon reading—but sitting in such a

space in Paris, I feel small beyond any measure. I'm waiting for Z. Our Italian cell phones don't work here, so we agreed to meet in front of Notre Dame at eleven, and it is past eleven by ten minutes, now twenty, now thirty. I don't know whether to stay or leave, or where I would go if I did, and I'm cold, wearing just a short, foolish dress under my long coat, and I want, for once, to be rid of this wanting, no longer as luminous as it seemed in the glittering dark of the bar, under the sun of Capri, no longer cinematic or meaningful but something I should be ashamed of, something I long ago should have shed. The romance that felt inevitable on the steps of my Florence apartment feels impossible in this cold moment, and I don't know what to do with the vacuous weight it's left behind. We waited too long, I think, and here I am, waiting longer still. I know, I know, that the great stones of the church before me are beautiful beyond description, but I can barely see them.

"Sappho begins with a sweet apple," Carson says, "and ends in infinite hunger."

Z. appears on the far side of the vast square, dark coat wrapped against the snow as he crosses toward me, apologizing—he got lost—and we make our way back to the Métro. On the subway, we sit across from each other in silence, looking out the same window at the occasional illumination of the tunnel's walls. My knees are tucked between his to fit in the cramped space of the subway car, and he rests a broad hand on them, light as the snow, shearing the space between us to the thinning nylon of my tights. He keeps it there until we reach our stop.

"We may need to have made an indelible mark on our lives," writes de Botton,

> to have married the wrong person, pursued an
> unfulfilling career into middle age or lost a loved

one before architecture can begin to have any perceptible impact on us, for when we speak of being 'moved' by a building, we allude to a bittersweet feeling of contrast between the noble qualities written into a structure and the sadder wider reality within which we know them to exist. A lump rises in our throat at the sight of beauty from an implicit knowledge that the happiness it hints at is the exception.

But exceptions are the stories I like to tell.

Z. knocks lightly on the door of my room. His room, I should say—his spare room, where I'm staying after three weeks of driving our country's highways, where I'm still half a day's drive from my own home, where I've just gone to bed after saying goodnight. It's been more than a year since we left Italy. Here, our part of the earth has turned to summer, and the stars are afire above the long American lake outside. "Come in," I say, sitting up, the sheet falling from my shoulders, and he does, leaving the door open behind him so that the light of the hallway falls in a long golden pattern on the darkened floor. He does, crossing that uncrossable space at last.

"Endeavoring to purchase something we think beautiful may in fact be the most unimaginative way of dealing with the longing it excites in us," writes de Botton, "just as trying to sleep with someone may be the bluntest response to a feeling of love." But I don't know this; I haven't read it yet.

"We could have done this in Paris," Z. says, rueful but smiling, his face half lit in the shadowed air above mine. But I can't let that regret through the door or it'll swallow the room, the house, the whole country.

"Better late," I say, leaving off the alternative. I'm not sure, even then, even now, that it is. *Never* is never-ending; the story gets to go on. But in the intimate collusion of that night, between walls whispering as if in conversation with the faint waves of the lake beyond, beneath a lamplit ceiling and atop Z.'s cast-off sheets—*We deserve a real bed*, he'd said, taking my hand to lift me from the narrow one in which I'd waited, leading me out the golden door and up the stairs—in the extended present of that night and day and night again, I let the words trail off.

We wake to rain. A thin window runs along the top of the wall, the whole length of the room, and the dense green of trees fills every inch of its matted frame. The leaves are as broad as those growing on cliffs above the Tyrrhenian Sea, etched with so much evidence of desire. I have let my longing be known, let it be asked and answered, and have not yet dissolved. There are my fingers, resting on his chest; there are his restless, gesturing hands at my back, in my hair, tracing the skin of my upturned wrist. The leaves shine in a downpour that shows no sign of abating, but we don't mind. We're happy to waste the day exquisitely inside.

In 1580 and 1581, Montaigne spent seventeen months traveling through Switzerland, Germany, and most of Italy, but his recorded observations of the latter rarely provide insight beyond his opinion of Italian women (not nearly as beautiful as rumored) and his ongoing struggle with kidney stones (awful). Louis Kahn's visit in late 1950 and early 1951, when he spent three months at the American Academy in Rome, seems far more influential; the Pantheon's concrete dome and light-filled oculus echo as loudly as my steps in the library's vertical expanse. "Mass and weight became especially important to him during this period," says Lesser, and "so did the materials that possessed and embodied these qualities, like brick and concrete . . . materials that not only emphasized their relation to gravity, but also displayed on their surface the process of their own making."

My office is full of such displays: the irregular meeting of mortar and brick on one wall, the cracked grain of wood on another, the circular indentations of tie-holes left visible in the concrete—others might have patched and filled them, but not Kahn. "The Pyramids try to say to you, *Let me tell you how I was made*," he says, and this building of his speaks with the same insistence. Reading Calvino's words between its walls, I begin to think that his fictional cities—Eudoxia, Perinthia—might be part of the same architectural tradition, not merely bearing the residue of their creation but continually enacting it: Let me tell you how I was made. Let me tell you how I am being made—still and now. They might not be cities after all, but simply billowing, shape-shifting visions seen and spoken by Polo and Khan, existent only if they're voiced. Let me tell you. Let me tell you.

Speaking of one such city or vision, Polo describes a bridge in meticulous detail, stone by stone. But Khan is in one of his darker moods, and he grows impatient with the meandering nature of the explorer's reports. "Why do you speak to me of the stones?" asks the emperor. "It is only the arch that matters to me."

"Without stones," says Polo, "there is no arch." The structure dissipates into parts; the story can't be told but in pieces. The process of their own making—brick and concrete and the cities of Calvino don't bother to hide their seams. "Although he returned to his work constantly, he hardly ever seemed to get the urge to cross things out, only to keep adding more," Bakewell says of Montaigne, explaining the notations scattered throughout most translations of the *Essays*, indicating later additions—always additions. "The *Essays* had grown alongside him for twenty years," says Bakewell. "The process could have gone on forever." For what else exists, but such a process? "There is no end in our inquisitions," writes Montaigne. "Our end is in the other world."

•

"There were people I wanted so much before I had them," writes the essayist Sarah Manguso, "that the entire experience of having them was grief for my old hunger." Perhaps I'm grieving still, all these years later, the absence of that hunger more gnawing, more wanting, than the hunger itself. How long will this mourning last? It occurs to me only now: how young he was, both then and then, though he always seemed certain and older (he was, by a few years). In Italy, I thought him worldly and otherworldly: my own personal Bacchus or Loki, an unsaintly saint smiling from the darkness, gesturing toward some irresistible unknown. An emblem among emblems. It's still unreal to me that he existed (and continues to exist) outside of that time and place. Sometimes it feels just as unreal that I did, and do.

"For Sokrates," writes Carson, "the moment when eros begins is a glimpse of the immortal 'beginning' that is a soul." In another book, Lesser quotes her subject: "I honor beginnings." So said Louis Kahn, whose sequence of love affairs was an open secret in his life: "Of all things, I honor beginnings." And Pavese, once more: *The only joy in the world is to begin.* A layer of terror runs under the sentence's lilt. The *only* joy? I know this isn't true, and yet.

Our beginning ends. How could it not? Away from Italy, yes, away from the spun top of every morning and every night the dark bar all to ourselves, far from the campfire around which we traded our stories of wolves and battles, swapped, for a moment only, our eyes and skies and desires—how could it not? But the place, or its absence, isn't wholly to blame. *The lover wants what he does not have*, Carson says. *It is by definition impossible for him to have what he wants if, as soon as it is had, it is no longer wanting.* The ancient stories ended when the lovers met, but ours doesn't; it can't. It merely becomes multiple, and they disentangle from each other, the brief knotting tugged away. *There is a dilemma within eros*, and we do not solve it.

•

"Like buildings," says de Botton, "we, too, contain opposites which can be more or less successfully handled." We want both brick and light; we are concrete and air. Well-balanced buildings, de Botton continues, serve "as exemplars of how we might adjudicate between the conflicting aspects of our characters, how we, too, might aspire to make something beautiful of our troubling opposites." I've grown less interested in the troubling opposites I didn't pick—my hypomania and depression, distant (at the moment) buffers of my happiness—and more concerned with the inclinations I do choose, or would if I could, conflicting as they are. I want the suspended beginning—of travel, of eros—and I want home, want the relationship sustained. I want the burning mystery of *St. John* and I want Montaigne in his tower room, all solid walls and ongoing work. The philosophers he loved, Bakewell writes, "agreed that the best path to *eudaimonia* was *ataraxia*, which . . . means equilibrium: the art of maintaining an even keel."

In the airy light and thick masonry of Kahn's library, haven't I struck such a balance? The steady day, the surprise of my work, the mind taking and creating its own reward—and at home, the love found five years ago still loved, still wanted, another kind of hunger. "They speak of visions of happiness," de Botton says of the places we make for ourselves: How greedy am I, to live in this vision, to long for that other? And another, and another. We hold so many different selves within, and yet I want so many more.

He lifts his hand from my knees and we leave the train. We walk the famous graves of Père Lachaise: I linger before Oscar Wilde's, Z. before Jim Morrison's. Afternoon has turned the flakes of snow to a fine mist, and the moisture seeps through our cheap coats and shoes. All the graveyards I've known back home are grassy and broad, the dead staking their vast, uncanny claim on meadows and churchyards, but here the stony paths run narrow and steep. Trees line every row, their branches stark against the pallid sky. The monuments, too, loom above us, heavy with their stone. "You perceive what you are," Carson says, "what you lack, what you could be." We've slipped out of time, I think, walking through this world shot in black-and-white. We've slipped out of the story we were telling, and I can't be sure anymore: if the city is real, if it ever was, if we only spoke it into existence. The cemetery is so quiet. The dead, like us, no longer speak.

There, in the absent past, I often had this feeling—I want to call it *architectural*, by which I mean both floating somewhere just above my head and yet clenching in my throat, my gut; I mean a thing both solid and full of space—I had this feeling like I'd arrived (or was arriving, or was about to arrive) on the other side of something, had passed through some door or veil as transformative as those in children's books: a whole world within, without. But there was another door or veil beyond, maybe, and another beyond that, always something ahead or above or to come. Or maybe there was just the one, one door or veil, but I kept entering and reentering, as if what I wanted lay always on the other side. The other side always what I wanted.

I'm trying to articulate this feeling; I'm also trying to regain it, to sustain it. If we are different people in different places, I want to be the girl I was there, again. I also want to remain myself. Perhaps we need only break Pavese's word in two to make the sentence more promising: *Life is not a search for experience but for our selves.* Our selves, all of them. If only we could gather and keep them, to be worn or stored as needed. Montaigne writes, Bakewell says, "about the sheer feeling of being alive," and though it's a simple phrase, I'm struck by it: *sheer* like that imagined veil, *sheer* like black tights. Something we can see through but dimly, can sweep aside. Something that hides and reveals all at once, that can be touched and keeps things from touching. Yes, you could describe this feeling of mine as *sheer*.

De Botton talks about "the memorial capacities of architecture," about the fact that so many significant structures, in ancient times and in our own, are built for funerary or commemorative purposes, made for the living but named for the dead. We build to help us remember. So go the tower rooms we construct of our lives: the books we collect, the gifts we keep, the simple words that merely read or overheard can cause whole scenes to spring and play on the curved wall of our memory: *stained glass, Notre Dame, lake.* "In truth," Bakewell admits, as I must, "however hard you try, you can never retrieve an experience in full." Her subject tried very hard indeed, not to retrieve a past experience but to relay, at every moment, his current one; Montaigne knew it—and the self living it—would be memory soon enough.

This written account—however galloping the *essai*—can never be equivalent to the lived experience nor even the lesser recollection, but it can make up for its deficiencies in other ways: art, insight, a belated and lasting surprise. Like a great building, it can offer both shelter and opening, can resist "a simplistic vision of who we might be," as de Botton puts it, in favor of "the labyrinthine reality of who we are." It's the labyrinth that attracts us, after all. "[O]f all that was mysterious," Bakewell says of Montaigne, "nothing amazed him more than himself, the most unfathomable phenomenon of all." But we *can* fathom ourselves, in the word's other meaning: not to understand a thing but to take its measure, whether we understand it or not. We can measure; we can sketch blueprints; we can build. We can reach out and touch another, saying, *Let me tell you how I was made.*

CONTINUOUS CITIES

Each of the cities is one city, goes the story. Each of the cities is Venice, Marco Polo's hometown. "Sire," Polo pleads with the emperor, after a long night of describing his explorations, "now I have told you about all the cities I know." But Khan knows this isn't true; he utters, himself, the name of the shining city built on a lagoon.

"What else do you believe I have been talking to you about?" Polo confesses. "Every time I describe a city I am saying something about Venice."

But when Khan presses him, insisting that he repeat the city's name at length, enumerating its qualities without omission or obfuscation, Polo resists. "Memory's images, once they are fixed in words, are erased," he says. "Perhaps I am afraid of losing Venice all at once, if I speak of it."

Perhaps I am afraid of losing Italy all at once, if I speak of it. This book took years to begin: false starts, false forms. Yet here we are, speaking, in the gardens of Kublai Khan, and the day is almost gone. *No one, wise reader, knows better than you that the city must never be confused with the words that describe it*—nor the words with the memory, the memory with the life. But there's little danger of that. I know the map is not the territory, but I love to run my fingers over it.

In 1271, a seventeen-year-old Venetian joined his merchant father and uncle on an expedition to places only vaguely sketched on the maps he'd seen. This young man—let's call him Marco, to distinguish him from his fictional counterpart—wouldn't return to his homeland for more than twenty years. He spent two decades traversing Asia and the Middle East, traveling farther—so the story goes—than any Westerner had before him, farther than any would for centuries to come. *The Travels of Marco Polo* claims, in its prologue, "that from the time when our Lord God formed Adam . . . down to this day there has been no man, Christian or Pagan, Tartar or Indian, or of any race whatsoever, who has known or explored so many of the various parts of the world and of its great wonders as this same Messer Marco Polo." In his introduction to the 1958 edition of these *Travels*, Ronald Latham concurs, calling the extravagant claim "a plain statement of fact."

Marco wrote the *Travels* in collaboration with Rustichello of Pisa, a romance writer with whom he shared a cell in Genoa near the end of the thirteenth century. (Marco had been captured by pirates and was being held as a prisoner of war.) The book's narration shifts as needed; Marco is often mentioned in the third person but occasionally in the first ("I, Marco Polo . . ."). For the most part, he's absent, less an author or even a character than a vessel for information: the names of cities, the customs of tribes, the geographies of countless steppes and rivers. He is "a somewhat colorless personality," Latham writes; Calvino took this absence like a sheet of glass and shone a great light through it. Calvino wrote the story we wish the *Travels* were, brimming with magic and imagination. "The book in which I think I've had the most to say remains *Invisible Cities*," he says in *Six Memos*, "a multifaceted structure in which each brief text sits close to others in a sequence that doesn't suggest causality or hierarchy but rather a network in which one can follow multiple paths and come to various ramified conclusions."

Still, I find traces of the later book in the work that inspired it: the details of cloth and crop, the seamless weaving of ostensible fact and anecdote, the geometric attention to the structures of buildings and the layouts of cities, and the endlessness of the cities themselves. They pile up on the page, and I understand the urge to sort them: thin cities, trading cities, cities and the sky. Similar, too, is each author's use of movement as transition, introduction, and elision all at once—Marco (or Rustichello) writes: "When the traveler leaves this city and journeys north-north-east for three days . . ."

So the *there* of Polo's first line—the place he leaves, the place from which he proceeds three days (or three months, or two decades) to the east—that *there* is probably here: these narrow canals and their unreal color, these stones damp beneath my feet. When Montaigne visited Venice in 1580, his secretary reports, "[H]e had found it different from what he had imagined, and a little less wonderful." I find Venice different from what I had imagined, but no less wonderful: water bright as turquoise where streets should be; gondolas floating by, open to the air; every building an improbable alignment of stone and sky. It doesn't stand on stilts, quite, nor dangle from strings, but the city is as striking as any of Calvino's. After all, it's one—or all—of them.

But I, I am far less wonderful here than I had imagined, far from the "elusively authentic self" described by Alain de Botton, despite the wondrous, inventive, resilient qualities written into the buildings around me. (Commissioned to design the Palazzo dei Congressi, the architect Louis Kahn offered to do it for free, saying:

"How could you charge for having your work in Venice?") I've traveled here with the ex-boyfriend I left behind when I came to Italy: he'd bought his plane ticket before we broke up, and I didn't want the money to go to waste. *Sure*, I'd said, when he asked if he should still come, and I was—sure that it would be fun, that it would be fine.

Now he's flown six thousand miles for a long weekend in Venice, and I wish—so intensely that my stomach cramps with the force of it—I wish I were alone. We are, for better or for worse, different people with different people, and I can't be my best self in his company. We'd begun dating nine months earlier, in the thick of my deepest-yet depression, when his interest in me cut through my deadened senses: his desire was something strong, something fierce, was *something*, at least, when I'd lived in a world of nothing for weeks. Unable to want anything myself, I let myself be wanted, as if my withered mind was some green thing surviving on instinct, leaning toward any light it could find. And he was kind, gentle and steady around the unpredictable force of my plummeting moods. I was happy—so the phrase goes—to let him take care of me.

But in Italy, I no longer need to be cared for. I no longer need to be wanted or comforted or merely kept afloat. Depression is another country, long abandoned, and the girl I was there a distant relative, little known and less in common. I know I should, but I can't bring myself to care about her.

Marco describes landscapes, city streets, and the vagaries of climate; he chronicles religious beliefs, criminal systems, and military capabilities; he makes note of acts of charity, marriage customs, eating habits, currencies, post-horses, superstitions, and oddities of every stripe: in one region, formal mourning persists for four years after a death; in another, dead boys and girls are joined in marriage by their families, so that they might share a household in the afterlife. ("They draw pictures on paper of men in the guise of slaves, and of horses, clothes, coins, and furniture, and then burn them; and they declare that all these become the possessions of their children in the next world.") And Marco (or Rustichello) relays this book-length barrage of statistics and idiosyncrasies in language studded with conversational asides—"You must know" and "Now let me tell you" and "You may take it for a fact"—as if all three hundred pages were relayed from one person to another over a campfire, or whispered in the sidelong space of a dingy bar, a tall tale for a long night.

In his introduction, Latham explains that this wandering style, full of asides and addendums, was common at the time of its writing, vital to "the art of the storyteller in an age when stories were few and time was plentiful." (Can you imagine?) The story needed to stretch, like a broth watered down, to feed so many for so long and not be spent. *Perhaps I am afraid of losing Venice all at once, if I speak of it*—so let's not speak all at once, but just a little at a time. "What more need I say?" Rustichello says, again and again—eight times alone in his prologue to Marco's book—but the question is never rhetorical. "What more need be said?" he says, and the answer is always: so much. The repeated words don't serve as conclusions but transitions, false peaks he raises only to carry us over. There's always another city, another custom, another curiosity, just a day's journey away. There's always something else *you must know*.

In *Invisible Cities*, Calvino transforms this conversational tone into pure conversation: following the revelatory mention of Venice, Khan and Polo address each other in the direct lines of a play's dialogue, men reduced to mouths—

> POLO: Perhaps this garden exists only in the shadow of our lowered eyelids, and we have never stopped: you, from raising dust on the fields of battle; and I, from bargaining for sacks

> of pepper in distant bazaars. But each time we
> half-close our eyes, in the midst of the din and
> the throng, we are allowed to withdraw here . . .
> to contemplate from the distance.

Perhaps we can, in fact, confuse the map for the territory, within the pages of the *Travels*, within the mysteries of *Invisible Cities*—perhaps we're meant to. In an essay, "The Traveller in the Map," Calvino reports on an exhibition of ancient maps and describes "the desire to live inside them, to grow small enough to find one's way amid the dense signs, to run through these maps, to lose oneself in them." He mentions the short story by Jorge Luis Borges, "On Exactitude in Science," about an imagined empire where the art of cartography grew so skillful and precise that a map was made on a scale of 1:1, the empire overlaid with its imitation.

The exhaustive catalog of Marco's *Travels* aims at such a scale, though it falls inevitably short. But in Calvino's novel, uninhibited by the strictures of nonfiction, I find a map of the empire that overtakes the empire, that becomes an empire unto itself. We could trace the directions given—*three days toward the east, a seven days' march through woodland, eighty miles into the northwest wind*—but I suspect we'd find ourselves drawing a circle or a spiral or a web, turning and returning to these continuous cities, the ones from which we've left. *What else do you believe I have been talking to you about?*

The cartography practiced by Calvino's characters is a fantastical one, to be sure, but it travels so far east of our lived experience that it catches up to it from the west, as if it traversed the whole finite, borderless surface of our world. Each page barters with the next, trading memory for desire, desire for signs, signs for the dead; each abstraction is translated, transformed into something as real as a handful of gems, a box of spices, a bolt of satin or silk. Here, right here, in the words spoken by Polo and Khan, is that *sheer feeling of being alive*, at times—our eyes half-closed in the midst of the din and the throng, one world without and another within. Vast lands stretch beyond our bodies, and vast lands beckon beneath our skin and skull: here be memory, here be desire. Which is the map and which is the empire? And which would you choose to linger and live in, could you separate them long enough to tell?

She threatens to return, that other, lesser self, in my ex-boyfriend's presence; he serves as an unwitting reminder of just how unhappy I can be. I can feel it coming, rising, water against the stone. But the strange experience of this watery once-republic can't be thwarted entirely by such a meager thing as my dissatisfaction, and some of the city's liquid pleasure seeps through. "[A]t certain hours," Polo says, of the city of Aglaura, "in certain places along the street, you see opening before you the hint of something unmistakable, rare, perhaps magnificent." In the equally fictional city of Venice, it's the last weekend of November, damp and cold, and other tourists are present only in diminishing numbers. The twisting alleyways we walk are empty, and the sudden expanse of St. Mark's Square seems, like the open spaces of Paris or Rome, built to be inhabited by creatures far larger than ourselves. We climb the cathedral's bell tower, and the lagoon unfurls below us: a hundred islands, two hundred canals, four hundred footbridges, and beyond it all, the distant sea grows close. In the silvered wind of this upper air, the city flattens into a map of itself, a map we can live within, as Calvino wished. I can imagine being unimaginably happy, here. Already, I want to return—next time, I'll be sure to get it right.

The extant names leap off the page, layered with meaning: Armenia, India, Baghdad. Without them, I'd forget these were real places visited by a real Marco eight centuries ago, and the book not merely an earlier draft of Calvino's fantasy. In his prologue, Rustichello calls the *Travels* a "Description of the World" and it was, as much as anything yet written had been. The book pushed past the bounds of the maps its author had followed, bushwhacking out into that *terra incognita* (*incognita*, at least, to him, and to me).

The *Travels* would lend its discoveries and descriptions to the maps in turn as, in the century following Marco's death in 1324, his long-left hometown came to dominate the flourishing field of cartography. In 1459, the Venetian monk Fra Mauro completed his world map—the "world" consisting of Europe, Asia, and Africa— the most expansive and most accurate rendering of that known world at the time. Mauro's remarkable creation relied on the reports of traveling merchants, even ones long dead: Marco's *Travels* provided some source material. Among the changes made to the planet by Fra Mauro was the banishing of Paradise: Eden, traditionally placed in the far East, was removed from the map altogether and depicted in a small, separate circle on the bottom of the page. Heaven was not, it turned out, a place on Earth—if it were, Marco surely would have visited it.

In "The Traveller in the Map," Calvino reminds us that the cartographical form most familiar to us today—"the map representing the earth's surface as though seen by an extraterrestrial eye"—is not the only one nor the simplest. Many early maps were scrolls, designed for the travel they facilitated. The Peutinger Table is just over a foot high and twenty-two feet long; this thirteenth-century copy of a Roman original depicts the continent-spanning network of the empire's roads: a Rand McNally for the Roman pilgrim. Gazing at Fra Mauro's densely elegant rendering of the world, I grow overwhelmed by its unknowability, but the Peutinger Table makes the world seem quite manageable, a journey we can measure in just one direction: days. "The need to contain within one image the dimension of time along with that of space is at the origins of cartography," says Calvino. "A geographical map, even though it is a static object, presupposes an idea of narrative; it is conceived on the basis of a journey; it is an Odyssey."

Narrative and linearity—"the succession of stops, the outline of a journey"—are assumed in literature, too, until they are upended; I didn't doubt that Polo's cities were different cities until Khan gave voice to his suspicion. But I too should have suspected something, should have sketched the map described and found it depicted a single point. "Irene is a name for a city in the distance, and if you approach, it changes," Polo says, in pages I've long left behind for my own. "There is the city where you arrive for the first time; and there is another city which you leave never to return. Each deserves a different name; perhaps I have already spoken of Irene under other names; perhaps I have spoken only of Irene."

Perhaps, he says, again and again: *Perhaps I am afraid, perhaps magnificent, perhaps I have spoken only . . .* The word's an unconscious favorite of mine, too: a tic or a failsafe or a flaw. Stories are no longer few, after all, and time has never been plentiful; I ought (perhaps?) to get on with it. But only after so many pages have I remembered: in English, the word shares a root with *happiness*. *Per*, meaning by, and *haps*, the plural of *hap*, meaning chance, as in *What are the haps?*, that affected variant of *What's happening?* or, more recently, *What's good?* What's good: vocabulary functions as optimism, eliding the possibility of less-good haps; *hap* blossoms into the *happiness* we ask after and long to hear. When *happy* first arose in English in the late fourteenth century, it meant lucky or fortunate, less an emotion than a state, and one beyond human control. Isn't it still? Happiness, an occurrence of chance: a happening, a happenstance. *Whatever happens will happen*, we say, a tautology meant to comfort. It doesn't.

•

You can wonder about or if or whether, or you can simply wonder at.
It's a Renaissance tradition, this wondering. In the centuries following Marco's adventures and Fra Mauro's mapmaking, adventure and
cartography blossomed together: reports of distant lands flooded
into and through seaports like Venice, and the maps expanded
accordingly. Copernicus had reminded Europe that our planet
revolves around the sun, and not the other way around, and the
planet itself was turning out to be a whole lot larger than imagined—and as full of wonders as Marco's *Travels* had promised, two
or three hundred years before.

The notion of a wonder cabinet emerged in the late sixteenth
century, as objects followed words along bustling trade routes and
shipping passages. Wealthy Europeans collected these objects—
strange plants, brilliant stones, the skulls and bones of unknown
animals, the art of other civilizations—and displayed them alongside their books and paintings, creating rooms that strove to hold
the world within. Today, we tend to keep our museums separate—art in one, natural history in another, drawing a distinction
between the works of humanity and the works of God, or science,
or happenstance—but wonder cabinets blurred such lines.

"I realize this is a museum," says a visitor to the present-day
Museum of Jurassic Technology, according to author Lawrence
Weschler in *Mr. Wilson's Cabinet of Wonder*, "but to me it's more
like a church." The two were interchangeable, in Italy: I visited
cathedrals with my art history class and made pilgrimages to l'Accademia. I scribbled notes and dates in the dark pews of churches
and in the bright light of museums, I practiced the kind of quiet
I mean when I say *pray*. In Venice, needing to renew this faith of
mine, this religion of happiness, I lingered before the shop window
displays of Murano glass—vases, dishes, rings—as reverently as
any believer. In Italian, *wonder* (n.) and *wonder* (v.) are related but

distinct, and different words are used for *wondering whether* and *wondering at*—but a single word overflows, holding all these meanings, in my native tongue. In Old English, the noun came first: *wonder* meant a thing before it meant the feeling that thing stirred in us. Sometimes, we need the thing: the blown glass, the map, the far-flung square. *Look*, we can say, our fingers pointing, our innermost hopes made tangible, *look at this wonder I've found*.

Consider this my wonder cabinet, my room piled high with evidence of elsewhere. If happiness is merely a matter of chance, well, my odds are better here. From a brochure available at the Museum of Jurassic Technology, discussing the American collector Charles Wilson Peale, Weschler shares the following: "Peale fervently believed that teaching is a sublime ministry inseparable from human happiness, and that the learner must be led always from familiar objects toward the unfamiliar—guided along, as it were, a chain of flowers into the mysteries of life."

A chain of flowers, then: the way every little bridge is mirrored in the water it crosses, making the city a double, its doppelgänger locked away below; the uncanny aquamarine of the water itself, as if part of another planet, shining by the light of some other sun; an ancient clock with a star at its center; a building glimpsed from the side, its foundation plunging straight into the waves; archways upon archways; steps that lead down from a door to the surface of the waiting lagoon, and then continue; underwater tunnels; bushes growing in both worlds at once; the hidden and then inescapable horizon; a stretch of pavement marbled like a god's enormous chessboard, waves lapping at its edge; bell towers and bright rooftops; the crucifixes atop them spindling away into the darkening sky; and a small porch of white stone that extends just a few feet out into the shining water and holds a lantern, a cloth-covered table, and a single chair. The evening's menu is laid open, just for you.

•

Polo constructs for Khan another kind of wonder cabinet, laying objects from his travels at the emperor's feet; he offers "ostrich plumes, pea-shooters, [and] quartzes" on one occasion, "drums, salt fish, [and] necklaces of wart hogs' teeth" on another. Or are these objects, like the cities from which they come, merely words pluming from the explorer's lips, illusory and vanishing? Are all the objects one object, its pages fluttering in the day's breeze? "I do not know when you have had time to visit all the countries you describe to me," Khan says. "It seems to me you have never moved from this garden."

That was hardly an impediment, in the twinned history of exploration and cartography. For every detailed rendering like Fra Mauro's, we can find a dozen shrugs in the direction of accuracy, hundreds of *terrae incognitae* happily left that way, countless forgeries and fabrications and fictions masquerading as fact. For every ostrich plume or warthog's tooth, the shelves of wonder cabinets held as many bones and skins and scales of basilisks, harpies, and dragons—or so their holders claimed. Such creatures winged and stormed in the corners of medieval maps, though the famous warning—*here be dragons*—is a mostly modern invention, found on just a single extant globe from the sixteenth century. Medieval and Renaissance cartographers hardly needed to warn their audience of monsters in far-off lands—what else would they expect to find?

"The visitor to the Museum of Jurassic Technology," Weschler writes, "continually finds himself shimmering between wondering at (the marvels of nature) and wondering whether (any of this could possibly be true)." So-called wonders might be exposed as fakeries, as humbugs. The humbug, like the wonder, is an object that conspires with its observer to create a feeling: of amazement, of suspicion, of a kind of happiness we might call delight. The object might be false, but that feeling—isn't it real? And though the thing might be the means, isn't the feeling what we're after?

"So then, yours is truly a journey through memory!" Khan snaps at Polo, tired of wondering, whether or at. "This is what I wanted to hear from you: confess what you are smuggling: moods, states of grace, elegies!"

Polo is unperturbed. If he's smuggling elegies, isn't one of them for the emperor? Hasn't Polo spoken Khan into being as surely as he's voiced so many cities? The other Marco performed this trick, in the *Travels*: "I have come to the point in our book at which I will tell you of the great achievements of the Great Khan now reigning," he says, "for everyone should know that this Great Khan is the mightiest man . . . who is in the world today or who ever has been, from Adam our first parent down to the present moment." But the present moment was 1298, and Kublai Khan was four years dead. Marco knew this, and hid it, a tremendous act of fiction in a book full of facts, a humbug that allows for so much wonder.

"[I]t's that very shimmer," Weschler continues, "the capacity for such delicious confusion . . . that may constitute the most blessedly wonderful thing about being human."

Venice is built of such shimmer and confusion. "The great cartographic center in the Renaissance," writes Calvino in "The Traveller in the Map," "was a city where the dominant spatial theme was uncertainty and variability, since the confines between earth and water there changed constantly: in Venice, the maps of the lagoon had to be updated constantly." No wonder, then, that Polo has to draw and redraw his word-made map of Venice: the city's contours, occupants, buildings, skyline, and even its name change with the tide. By the time he offers Khan one description, the place described has transformed, turning his words into lies. He can't keep up; he can only circle. "What develops in the great novels of the twentieth century is the idea of an *open encyclopedia*," Calvino says in *Six Memos*. He doesn't apply the idea to his own work, but I will, finding *Invisible Cities* buried in this line: "[A]ny totality," he says, "that is not potential, speculative, or plural is no longer thinkable."

On our last day in Venice, we wake to sirens outside the window, shrill in the still-dark of early morning, and fall back to sleep. When we wake and rise hours later, the darkness has given way to a pearl-gray sky and the canal-side walkway below our room has flooded, the confine between this particular stretch of earth and water revealed as flimsy, arbitrary, and now erased. A few Venetians stride in thigh-high waders through the new-made sea—white stone glowing below the water separates the passable depths of the one-time sidewalk from the canal to which it's surrendered—but our cheap, foreign shoes are no match for the moat that surrounds us. I can't help taking nature's indifference personally, finding a perfect metaphor in the rising flood and my own pitiful unease. My desire to visit a different Venice—one where I'm happy, alone, finding poems in Fra Mauro's map, in the Murano glass, in the pews of St. Mark's—this wish is met by resounding denial: I can't even leave the building. I can't leave the company of this man I no longer want to be wanted by, nor this self I've traveled so far, so fast, so constantly—*running breathlessly, and not yet arrived*—to escape. The city's singular beauty has grown ugly in excess; the very strangeness I came to see now keeps me from seeing anything but the narrow view from a single window, all those potentials washed away. I open the window to smoke a cigarette, and a cold wind rushes in from the flooded world.

Acqua alta, the Venetians call the regular rising of the lagoon, but this high tide has been augmented by days of rain and wind. At some point in the last hours of the morning, the water reaches its greatest height in more than twenty years; only three times in recorded history has the sea lapped higher against the city's walls. When it falls low enough for us to leave, late in the afternoon, and carry our bags over the soaked stones to the train station, we watch shopkeepers mop out their stores, objects piled high on tables and shelves within. Trash bags lifted by the tide have been deposited in the middle of squares and sidewalks, and a thick silt fills the cracks between the cobblestones. Its grains stick to the peeling soles of my boots.

"I speak and speak," Polo says to Khan, "but the listener retains only the words he is expecting. The description of the world to which you lend a benevolent ear is one thing . . . another, that which I might dictate late in life, if I were taken prisoner by Genoese pirates and put in irons in the same cell with a writer of adventure stories." The real intrudes on the written, as we approach the end of *Invisible Cities*; the fictional Polo admits (within a glorious subjunctive) his awareness of the real one. Marco inhabits both Polo's past and his future, for the traveler who spins his stories in the presence of Kublai Khan has not yet finished his years of service to the emperor, has not yet left him, not yet returned to the West; Khan is not yet dead, and the *Travels* not yet written. The garden where the book takes place (if it takes place anywhere) is one more continuous city, unable to be fixed and held in time—*time*, another meaning offered by the Old English word from which *tide* takes its root. Our lives are charted, like the sea, by the heights of their rise, the depths of their fall.

What more need I say? Khan and Polo map and remap their shifting cities, filling them—as ancient cartographers did—with visions and hopes and whispered fears. Every place exists in a hundred different ways; there are a dozen different versions (*potential, speculative, plural*) of Marco's original *Travels*. "Although manuscripts of Polo's work exist in most of the languages of Western Europe,"

Latham writes, "not one of these can be regarded as complete; and even by fitting them all together like the pieces of a jigsaw puzzle we cannot hope to reconstitute the original text." His edition is dotted with shorthand, pointing the reader to these many versions—manuscript F, manuscript L, and V, and R, and so on—each addendum a reminder of how much *terra* remains *incognita* to us.

"[T]he unknown is always more appealing than the known; hope and imagination are the only consolations for the disappointments and sorrows of experience," Calvino writes in *Six Memos*. "Man thus projects his desire onto the infinite, feeling pleasure only when he can imagine that it won't end. But since the human brain can't grasp the infinite"—or, as physicist Carlo Rovelli might remind us, the infinite is an illusory concept, destined for disproval—"it must content itself with the indefinite." (*Indefinite*, like the article: *a* happiness, as Pavese has it, just one of many we might find.) So we love to wonder at; we love to wonder whether. We thrill to the edges described by Anne Carson, most enticing when they blur. We linger before Leonardo's enigmatic smiles, Michelangelo's rough and undone marble, a dome only dreamt of for a hundred years. Longing to live in such moments of suspension, we dream ourselves: a city built on shifting waters, a city that can float. Impossible thing! But there it is, solid stone holding up our own solid feet.

What more need be said? There was the game we played as children in my cousins' pool, closing our eyes to the bright, too-light sheen of the water and calling the traveler's name. The game was a variation of tag, with It blinded like Polyphemus, or a kind of hide-and-seek, with only one place to hide. The rules were simple and stringent, but someone always cheated to escape, hoisting herself out of the water after one call-and-response, sprinting the hot concrete length of the pool, and slipping soundlessly into the other end before the next shout came: *Marco!* It was terrible, to be the one whose eyes had to remain closed, shut to the wondrous sparkle of the pool, and the water growing cold around you. You felt, indeed, like a wanderer in a strange land, like a prisoner held by pirates. *Marco!* you'd cry, as if calling for a parent, but no parent ever came. Only the distant replies—*Polo! Polo! Polo!*—as if the two men—real and imagined, buried and resurrected, remembered and retold—long to speak at last only to each other, no need of emperors or interlocutors, just two halves of a knucklebone returned together, two bodies that used to be one. As if they have spotted each other across the vast plains of a great continent and raised their arms in greeting, shouting in recognition—*Marco! Polo!*—as they approach, twin silhouettes shimmering like a mirage, like a city they might come home to, after so many years away.

HIDDEN CITIES

B ACK IN FLORENCE, December swings down from the distant
mountains and we grow into our coats. I spend these weeks
writing papers, taking tests, trying to make the wine on which I
spend the last of my savings stretch; we sip slowly, passing bottles
with gloved fingers on the steps of Santa Croce. Annie and I walk
to Ponte Santa Trinita at sunset, climbing over the short wall that
lines the bridge to sit on a cement pylon jutting out into the Arno.
Light plays its probabilities on the thick felt of the sky, blue giving
way to long shots of pink and red, and the air darkens on our bare
and upturned faces. In the bar, Z. and I listen to the singer for a final
time and hug him goodbye, promising to return. We smoke on the
stoop next door, across from the café named for Dante's doomed lovers, and pretend we're not so cold, though we lean together against
the city's first flakes of snow. They are fine and do not last, melting
under the white lights that have been strung along each avenue.
Florence glitters like the mirage it's always been.

"Beauty is nothing other than the promise of happiness,"
says the author Stendhal, who lends his name to a psychosomatic

reaction—Stendhal syndrome—caused by an excess of that beauty, by too much exposure to art and wonder. The writer suffered such an episode—"I was seized with a fierce palpitation of the heart; the wellspring of life was dried up within me, and I walked in constant fear of falling to the ground"—upon visiting Florence in 1817, upon walking the streets and entering the churches I've spent three months among. Another name for this reaction is Florence syndrome—Florence syndrome and *la malattia del duomo*, one ailment caused by the city's presence and the other by its absence. I would endure the former for a lifetime, I think, as the wind rises off the river and the sun vanishes into the hills; I would suffer it gladly—happily.

But I'm losing hold of this pretense, this present tense, not present for years now. I found it hard to feel present even then, in those last few weeks in Florence: we thought and spoke only of the future, when we would—without a doubt—return. What good was the present to us? The weeks when it seemed unending had passed; the past had grown weighty, scavenging every second for itself; and we begrudged time this clumsy disappearing act. A mean trick, I thought, and think.

In "Happily," the poet Lyn Hejinian writes, "Nostalgia is another name for one's sense of loss at the thought that one has sadly gone along happily overlooking something, who knows what." The period is mine—Hejinian leaves the line to gape and waver. *Who knows what* . . . Not me, surely. If I knew what I have overlooked (and still), we'd both be spared the length of these pages. *The past is not for living in*, John Berger says, but how I have loved this visit, spread thin as it is.

Marco Polo is trying to make Kublai Khan understand the harmonics by which cities are not merely built but composed. Khan imagines wonders of architecture and landscape, maps gridded streets and rivers, plants flora and summons fauna, but Polo stops him with a gentle reprimand. All cities, the explorer insists, need "a connecting thread, an inner rule, a perspective, a discourse."

"Cities," Polo says, "like dreams, are made of desires and fears."

Khan scoffs. What could an emperor desire or fear? He wants for nothing, and nothing threatens him. (Or so the emperor—aging, the world encroaching—must maintain.) He is impregnable as a city himself, self-contained and unyielding. But Polo insists: "You take delight not in a city's seven or seventy wonders, but in the answer it gives to a question of yours."

"Or the question it asks you," Khan admits, "forcing you to answer, like Thebes through the mouth of the Sphinx."

What question did I ask of Florence, or it of me? What answer did I get or give?

First, let's consider another question: Who narrates *Invisible Cities*? In its opening pages, before Polo puts a single foot toward Diomira, Calvino sets the scene for the conversation to come: "In the lives of emperors there is a moment which follows pride in the boundless extension of the territories we have conquered, and the melancholy and relief of knowing we shall soon give up any thought of knowing or understanding them." *The territories* we *have conquered*— even I can catch the grammar of the Italian, the first-person plural *abbiamo conquistato*. The narrator counts himself among these emperors: Has Khan been telling this story all along, remembering Polo's remembrances or inventing upon his inventions? Is Polo, like his cities, just a dream of the sleeping emperor, adrift in his garden? Or is the author another emperor—*we* being him and Khan, compeers—and these pages but the territories he once conquered, and now must rule? He leaves them in his wake like battlefields.

We shall soon give up any thought of knowing them—soon, I think, but not yet. In this striving to understand where we've been and where we've gone, another kind of pleasure takes root. The past, the memory—they demand our attention, and the product of that attention becomes its own past, its own memory, and makes its own demands in turn. We might continue in this way for quite a while. "Constantly I write this happily," says Hejinian, the adverbs like bookends, a matching set: they go together. *Constantly, happily.* Aristotle would approve of this manifestation of happiness, no abstract noun but a thing always linked to a verb, found only in action. So we act, we grasp, we gesture. Zeno's race can never be won, but that's no reason not to run it; words fail, but that's no reason not to speak. The *Travels* are not the travels and the words are not the city, but the space created between the two might be lovely enough to make Stendhal faint. The air was merely air, after all, until the reaching fingers of Adam and God made it an edge, electric.

How to live: my question might be this plain, as old as Montaigne, as Aristotle, as the nameless ranks that came before. Or a variant thereof: How to be happy? How to stay happy? How to bring back a happiness, found and lost? How to stave off a darkness that loiters and returns, that I can't seem to lock in one place and leave behind? How can my mind move quickly enough to escape—like one of Leonardo's scribbled machines, powered by its own motion—when my body is confined to one city, one season at a time? Can happiness ever linger, lengthening from action to place, somewhere to be lived in instead of sought? Where is that place? Where is it? And when?

Another question: What's *invisible* about these cities? The word doesn't spring to my fingertips when summing up the conversations of Polo and Khan. I've called his cities *imagined, invented,* and *impossible*, but none of these is the word Calvino chose. His adjective insists on a premise opposite to mine: these places are not imagined, not impossible, but firmly located in the realm of existence—they're merely unseen.

By whom? Khan, for one. If we take the novel at its word, the cities Polo has visited are surely invisible to the emperor, stuck in his palatial state of unknowing. His territories can appear to him only dimly, at a great distance, composed not of brick and stone but of the Venetian's sentences and pantomimes.

Perhaps the cities are invisible to Polo, too; they might exist somewhere he's never been and can only guess at, his speculation conquering as many miles as the Great Khan's finest riders. Perhaps the streets and docks and strung laundry he describes in such detail are scavenged from other travelers and never so much as glimpsed by the emperor's favorite merchant; perhaps he has traveled thus far and no farther, mired in the delights of Xanadu. We've been given hints of this possibility: Doesn't Polo see metropolises like Olinda, Marozia, and Theodora only with his eyes half-closed, reclining in Khan's garden? (Or is it Khan's garden that exists only behind the explorer's eyelids?)

The cities are invisible to me, to you. And so I assume their nonexistence, their invention, just because I've never stepped through the pipe-lined paths of Armilla or mourned the dead buried below Eusapia. But they're *there*, Calvino promises, hiding behind the eyelids or before them, unseen but not unreal. The struggle is ours: how to explore these alleyways, when we cannot see their cobbles? How to wander these squares, if we don't know where they end? How can we trust enough to search for a city we can't glimpse? How could we find it, blind as we are? How would we live within its walls?

I know there lies futility in this longing—for elsewhere, for elsewhen. I know the transformation promised by travel and nostalgia—

that word rooted in *homesickness*, just another *malattia*—can be as superficial as that hoped for in a haircut, a new pair of shoes, the ingredients bought aspirationally, the books piled high on the night-stand, unread. Our selves are many but inescapable; we can't change our faintest, inerasable contours. And yet the inveigling possibility, however impossible, that we *might*—perhaps this sense of possibility itself, rather than any of the futures it builds like cities in our minds, is the place where we are happiest. "Is happiness the name for our (involuntary) complicity with chance?" Hejinian asks, returning the word to its roots: happening, happenstance. "Anything could happen," she writes, and I'm reminded of my own tentative hope: *Believing I might, at any time, be surprised by happiness—isn't this a kind of happiness itself?* Perhaps such belief is not just one place where happiness might flourish, but the only place it can be found. Is this an answer, or another question? They grow indistinguishable, linked like Leonardo's favorite set of gestures: the pointing finger and the smile. Like a long glance, like a kiss, they ask and answer all at once.

Khan was real too, of course: really Kublai (or Kubilai, or Khubilai), the warlord grandson of Genghis become emperor of China and beyond. "In the courtyard of his palace at Khan-balik . . . he sowed seeds of prairie grass to remind him of the freer world from which he had come," says Ronald Latham; Eliot Weinberger writes in "Khubilai Khan at the Met" that "he preferred to sleep in a yurt on the palace grounds." Though Coleridge and Calvino will take him for their own, making him the architect of a dreamscape and the interviewer of a figment, he doesn't know this yet, nor mind. He rides through that prairie grass like a man aflame: his breath heavy, his skin alight under the sun he's sure, one day, to own. One fifth of this boundless earth is his.

And you're real too, wise reader, aren't you? My eyes have been half-closed all this time—one world within, another without—and

I forget which words I've spoken, which I've merely imagined speaking. Forgive me. I've spread my cities at your feet, my warthog's teeth and ostrich plumes, but you—you've seen cities too, I know. Your happiness is another world entire.

And my happiness? Where is it? After all this time, where have I tracked it?

Memory says happiness lies in a place, *is* a place—you know where, memory says. Happiness is a country of stone streets and great cathedrals set amid the hills; of the bright shout of sunlight rising from each river, soaking through the windows of each gleaming morning train; of seamed marble and olive groves and laughter like wine on your tongue—or was it wine like laughter? Hard to tell whether you poured the place down your throat or built its walls with every exhalation. Better check, memory says: you can go back at any time and find it, waiting. You need only book a ticket. You need only close your eyes.

Desire says happiness lies in a person—oh, any old person, desire says, and hums its constant song over the sound of my protestation. Desire is a shapeshifter: now a broad wink, now a rising smile, now shoulders lifting from white sheets. Desire rests its hand on my shivering knees. Touch me, desire says, touch me, touch me—but I know better than that. Do you really? desire asks, and trickster that it is, I almost don't recognize it—I almost say *no*. That is, I almost say *yes*.

Signs point to other signs, symbols to more symbols. Happiness lies in this translation, they say, in an accumulation of meaning, a spawning of knowledge, a proliferation of syllables—if you can only find the right collective noun, surely it will contain your happiness, that furred or flighty thing. If you can only find the right book, the right sculpture, the right formula or fact, if you can only piece together the countless tesserae, golden as the days. You'd better get started, the signs say.

Happiness is thin, the cities say, so thin you can see through it, floating in the sea. Happiness is as clear as glass, as goggles, as the lenses of microscopes and telescopes, as the bottom of your wine glass, lifted and drained: a way of seeing, and not the object seen. You're always confusing the two, they admonish. Happiness is closer than you think. But whatever you do, don't go reaching for it—you'll only smudge it with your greedy fingers. Whatever you do, the cities say, and their voices grow dark with warning, opaque—whatever you do, don't touch.

No, say the trading cities, happiness lies in touching, in communion, in the dissolving air between hands and mouths, in the words they speak and gesture, words you can carry, words you can keep. Happiness is like money, only worth what it can gather. So gather what you can, voracious, and keep it close. Stockpile your happiness: you know well enough that there are lean months yet to come.

Eyes spy my happiness lingering just beyond the painting's edge. They point the way—why can't I follow? You're getting warmer, they say, as I scour the warp and weft and back of every canvas, lifting the frame away from the wall. Warmer, warmer.

Names say happiness lies in shedding mine. Grow anonymous, they whisper, grow alone. You've been nothing but a body occupying a window seat, nothing but a mind churning away. Weren't you happy, then? they ask, but I swear, I can barely remember—was that even me? Take our word for it, the names say. This happiness—it isn't for the meek, you know. What have you done to earn it? To find it? I mean, have you even *looked*? The names shake their great, lovely heads in disappointment, and slip away.

The dead, they don't say much.

The sky says, silly girl, your happiness is everywhere: in these open windows, in these turrets rising, the clouds frothing just for you. Your happiness is the sun, present even when you can't see it. It tugs your little planet along on its tether; it burns up the blackness, ecstatic. Can't you feel its warmth on your face? Can't you feel its weight, pulling at your blood? It might be indefinite, your happiness, but it's not indefinable. Go on, give it a try. The sky smiles wide. Don't worry, it says, your happiness can't be squandered. Does the sun shine any less brightly because the bricks soak up its heat? Write all the words you want, says the sky, and tell me how it was.

There's no such thing as happiness, the continuous cities say. There's only this. And they gesture up and down, toward, around. But the maps made by their ancient fingers depict a scroll rolled shut, a world grown flat, all dragons and no paths. Every time I set out, I end up back where I began.

"My intention was to allow for the influx of material that surges into any thought, material that is charged with various and sometimes even incompatible emotional tonalities," Hejinian says, speaking of "Happily." "These emotional tonalities make it impossible to say with certainty that one is happy, for example, just as they make it impossible to say that one is not. That is, one is never solely happy."

As with people, so with the cities that bear their names. In Raissa, for example, Calvino writes, "at every second the unhappy city contains a happy city unaware of its own existence." Or consider the final city described or imagined or guessed at by Polo and Khan, a city that branches endlessly: "[T]he real Berenice is a temporal succession of different cities, alternately just and unjust . . . [and] all the future Berenices are already present in this instant, wrapped one within the other, confined, crammed, inextricable." They're discomfiting, these cities, but they offer comfort too: *they make it impossible to say that one is not.* Among those many tangled Berenices, mustn't some of them hold wonders beyond our grandest imagining? Of the many selves roiling beneath our skin, mustn't some of them be happy? "Make them endure," Polo says to Khan, the last words exchanged between these friends of many years: "Make them endure, give them space."

Eros is lack, says Anne Carson, and what more is memory, what else the dead? An absence lies at the heart of every approach: in the promise of each new thought, a reaching. Memory, desire, signs, eyes, names, the dead, the sky—they founder and flourish along Carson's edges, along Pavese's essentials, all these *things tending toward the eternal or what we imagine of it*. Like language, they stand in for something else, something missing—and yet, without that absence, why would we bother to talk? Our minds can fire by such thin fuel. "Simultaneous pleasure and pain are its symptom," Carson says of eros, and I want to expand her definition extravagantly, make it wide enough to cover life itself: "Lack is its animating, fundamental constituent. As syntax, it impressed us as something of a subterfuge: properly a noun, [it] acts everywhere like a verb. Its action is to reach, and the reach of desire involves every lover in an activity of the imagination."

So we imagine: other selves, other cities, a hundred variants of happiness. And when we find our imaginings in a room entered or a landscape glimpsed—what a gift. What luck, what chance, that I found such a happiness so brightly drawn, and for so long. My cheeks still flush at the mention—on any given page, in any conversation—of *Florence, Ravenna, Riomaggiore, Capri*, these names like the many capitals of a country found nowhere on Earth, homeland of my happiness. I imagine we each keep such an atlas-turned-dictionary, names expanding into entries, into—as we say—what they *mean*. I still order Sangiovese from any wine list I find it on, less a matter of taste than of allegiance. Once, every glass held more than wine within—held an autumn sun, a sea wind, porticos and domes—as weighty and vast as the squares and buildings of Renaissance cities. The taste is the same, and though sights, sounds, and scents might differ, I take the wine on my tongue as a reminder: happiness, like an invisible city, requires a kind of belief. It's there, somewhere, whether I see it or not. I can stand on its hidden stones, if I only put enough faith in my feet.

The last thing written in the notebook I kept while in Italy is a quote: "Paul was thrown to the ground that he might be lifted up." The line is unattributed, though I always make note of such things. Where did these words come from? *Paul was thrown to the ground that he might be lifted up.* This is the narrative we know, told by psychology and Catholicism, by Dante and Camus. This narrative runs through so many of the stories we tell ourselves: we endure great pain as a means to some future joy. This is the metaphor I've packed my own small pain into, a way to carry it for so long: I trade the depths plumbed in depression for the heights reached upon its release. "I consider it an anthropological constant," Calvino writes in *Six Memos*, "this nexus between the levitation desired and the deprivation suffered."

But we already know this story. I don't need to hear it, nor tell it, anymore. We know too well why Paul was thrown to the ground—*that he might be lifted up.*

But why was he lifted up? Why was I? To what end, this happiness?

"Unlike each detail happiness comes to no end, no good but that of something like the mouth in the windblown treetops shaping a sound," writes Hejinian, and I turn my ear to the page, listening. "There is no better correspondence."

In the same notebook—from a paragraph written in the summer before Florence, a paragraph meant for a novel never finished—a character, traveling, wonders: *How to keep it up? How did one stay happy?* Funny, how these things burrow and germinate. We could have started anywhere, you see, and any ending we might find is but a temporary pause. The story goes on. The map turns out to be a circle, or a spiral, or a web. Each city holds a million more within it, and *there is no end in our inquisitions: our end is in the other world.* Elsewhere, elsewhen—shall we go?

The courtyard is green and flowering, still, in the warm afternoon of early autumn. The leaves haven't yet begun to turn. Every hour spreads wide to allow time for espresso in small, white cups; feet up on each other's chairs; arms bare as if to catch the sun within them. My fingers learn the hand-made language of another's, twisting thin paper around sweet tobacco, licking shut what I'll soon breathe in. *No better correspondence.* It seems conceivable that I might taste the world this way: wrapping it up, bringing it to my lips. Birds I can't name riot in the trees nearby. We speak (*constantly, happily*), words that will fly away but leave a winging knowledge in their wake, like a place to come back to. Like a city, maybe, a city with a dome, with narrow, winding streets and sky-bright squares. And if that city were to ask, forcing me to answer—*What is it, this happiness you're always going on about?*—I'd reply only with a gesture: arms out, palms up, my whole body caught inhaling. Eyes and shoulders lifting, never to fall. This, my hands would say. And the day is clear and blue between my fingers.

ACKNOWLEDGMENTS

I'm indebted beyond measure to the translators whose work I quote under other names: Edward MacCurdy and Jean Paul Richter (Leonardo), G. H. Noehden (Goethe), Anne Carson (Sappho, Plato), Simon Carnell and Erica Segre (Rovelli), Mark Musa (Dante), Blomfield Jackson (Arius), J. Solomon (Aristotle), R. W. Flint, Jeanne Molli, and A. E. Murch (Pavese), Justin O'Brien (Camus), Harry Zohn (Benjamin), Anthony Mortimer (Michelangelo), John Florio (Montaigne), Ronald Latham (Polo, Rustichello), Haakon Chevalier (Stendhal), and, of course, Geoffrey Brock, Martin McLaughlin, and especially William Weaver (Calvino).

The greatest of thanks go to Jill Meyers and everyone at A Strange Object/Deep Vellum. I began writing *The Traces* while working at Literati Bookstore, and I'm grateful to Mike and Hilary Gustafson for creating that beautiful space and supporting my work, in every sense of the word. I finished the book while serving as the George Bennett Fellow at Phillips Exeter Academy, an incomparable year. For gifts of space and funding before and since, I'd like to thank

MacDowell, the Vermont Studio Center, the Kimmel Harding Nelson Center for the Arts, the Minnesota State Arts Board, and the Helen Zell Writers' Program at the University of Michigan. I've spent my working life in independent bookstores and public libraries, and my thanks go out to all who keep such institutions alive.

I'm grateful for the generosity of my teachers, especially Todd Hearon, Maggie Dietz, Claudia Rankine, Charmaine Craig, the much-missed Peter Greer, and the great David Weber, from whom I continue to learn. I'm grateful to Jia Tolentino and Brit Bennett for lending their keen eyes to this manuscript, and to Carrie Dedon, early reader and art consultant extraordinaire. And I'm grateful to Chris McCormick, who read the first draft and the last draft and never doubted, despite all the years between, that those drafts would someday be a book. Thank you for keeping the faith.

ABOUT THE AUTHOR

Mairead Small Staid is a writer from Massachusetts. Her work has appeared widely, including in *AGNI*, the *Believer*, and the *Paris Review*, and has earned awards from MacDowell, the University of Michigan, and Phillips Exeter Academy, where she was the George Bennett Fellow. *The Traces* is her first book.

ABOUT A STRANGE OBJECT

Founded in 2012 in Austin, Texas, A Strange Object champions debuts, daring writing, and striking design across all platforms. The press became part of Deep Vellum in 2019, where it carries on its editorial vision via its eponymous imprint. A Strange Object's titles are distributed by Consortium.

Available now from A Strange Object

PARTNERS

Walmart  pixel texel

ALLRED
CAPITAL MANAGEMENT
of
RAYMOND JAMES®

LIFE
IN DEEP ELLUM

EMBREY FAMILY
FOUNDATION

COMMON
DESK
COWORKING

ADDITIONAL DONORS, CONT'D

Kelly Falconer
Kevin Richardson
Laura Thomson
Lea Courington
Lee Haber
Leigh Ann Pike
Lowell Frye
Maaza Mengiste
Mark Haber

Mary Cline
Max Richie
Maynard Thomson
Michael Reklis
Mike Soto
Mokhtar Ramadan
Nikki & Dennis Gibson
Patrick Kukucka

Patrick Kutcher
Rev. Elizabeth & Neil Moseley
Richard Meyer
Sam Simon
Sherry Perry
Skander Halim
Sydneyann Binion
Stephen Harding

Stephen Williamson
Susan Carp
Theater Jones
Tim Perttula
Tony Thomson

SUBSCRIBERS

Andrea Pritcher
Anthony Brown
Aviya Kushner
Ben Fountain
Brian Matthew Kim
Caroline West
Caitlin Jans
Courtney Sheedy
Elena Rush

Elif Ağanoğlu
Erin Kubatzky
Eugenie Cha
Gina Rios
Ian Robinson
Joseph Rebella
Kasia Bartoszynska
Kenneth McClain
Lance Salins

Margaret Terwey
Matthew Eatough
Michael Lighty
Michael Schneiderman
Ned Russin
Ryan Todd
Shelby Vincent
Stephen Fuller

AVAILABLE NOW FROM DEEP VELLUM

FORTHCOMING FROM DEEP VELLUM